Letters to AMERICAN CHRISTIANS

Letters to AMERICAN CHRISTIANS

JOHN K. STONER & LOIS BARRETT

A Christian Peace Shelf Selection

HERALD PRESS
Scottdale, Pennsylvania
Kitchener, Ontario

Library of Congress Cataloging-in-Publication Data
Stoner, John K., 1942-
    Letters to American Christians / John K. Stoner and Lois
Barrett. p. cm.
    "A Christian peace shelf selection."
    ISBN 0-8361-3496-6 (pbk. : alk. paper)
    1. Peace—Religious aspects—Christianity. 2. Christianity and
justice. I. Barrett, Lois. II. Title.
BT736.4.S78 1989
261.8'73—dc20   89-2170
                                                                          CIP

♾️ ™

The paper used in this publication meets the minimum require-
ments of American National Standard for Information Sciences—
Permanence of Paper for Printed Library Materials, ANSI Z39.48-
1984.

LETTERS TO AMERICAN CHRISTIANS
Copyright © 1989 by Herald Press, Scottdale, Pa. 15683
    Published simultaneously in Canada by Herald Press,
    Kitchener, Ont. N2G 4M5. All rights reserved.
Library of Congress Catalog Card Number: 89-2170
International Standard Book Number: 0-8361-3496-6
Printed in the United States of America
Design by Paula M. Johnson

1 2 3 4 5 6 7 8 9 10 96 95 94 93 92 91 90 89

*To the children
of the twenty-first century*

Contents

Foreword by Ronald J. Sider 9
Preface 11

1 Does God Save from Enemies? 15
2 A Disarming Initiative by Jesus 35
3 Social Justice and Spirit Renewal 53
4 Conversion to the Kingdom of God 71
5 Christian Peacemaking 87
6 Your Vocation and God's Creation 105
7 Peace Church Evangelism 122
Afterword 135

Christian Peace Shelf 136
The Authors 140

Foreword

Letters to American Christians is simple, clear, and powerful. It has that profound simplicity that goes directly to the heart of an issue. It has the clarity of a pristine mountain stream. And it has the power of biblical truth boldly contrasted with contemporary failure, foolishness, and sin.

Letters to American Christians is a ringing call to reconsider Jesus' command to love our enemies. Grounded in the Scriptures and historic Christian faith, the book is thoroughly evangelical.

It is also as relevant as this morning's newspaper headlines. I recommend this book to Christians who call themselves pacifists and Christians who identify with the just-war tradition. Pacifists will find here a vigorous, pointed statement of the radical costly position that they claim to affirm and so often fail to live. This book will serve pacifists both as a challenging refresher course in what they believe and also as a useful popular tool for sharing their position with others.

Christians in the just-war tradition will find here a disturbing prod to ask again whether they have not too quickly passed over the possibility that Jesus summons his followers to a radically different approach to enemies.

Although it contains profound theological reflection, this book is not intended as a scholarly treatise. It does not pretend to be a theological refutation of the just-war doctrine or a detailed exegetical defense of pacifism. The authors know those books well and refer the reader to them in the bibliography. Rather, *Letters to American Christians* is crisp popularization of a high order.

I would not put every sentence exactly as the authors do. But then I don't agree totally with even my best friends. And one of the authors has been one of my closest friends for many years. As a close friend who has walked with John over the years, I can witness that he practices what he preaches. He lives simply, adores the crystal streams and mountain grandeur of God's glorious creation, and immerses his life in prayer and solitude.

At almost every point, however, I believe this book is right on target. Its clear, succinct biblical message is urgently needed in our churches. If heeded, its message would transform our society the way the simple, daring faith of the early Christians conquered a pagan world.

—*Ronald J. Sider*
Professor of Theology and Culture
Eastern Baptist Theological Seminary

Preface

Dear Christian Friends in America:

This book is a collection of letters to you. The letters are addressed to you not only as individuals, but to you as Christian churches. Just as the apostles wrote letters to the churches in the first century of the Christian era, so we are writing to the churches about a crisis that confronts our country, our world, and our churches. That crisis is the nuclear arms race. We write because we believe the solution to that crisis lies in a new understanding of who Jesus is and of the salvation Jesus brings to the world.

In our prayers we thank God for you and for your commitment to the Lord. But we hear many people using the name of Jesus in ways that do not reflect the Jesus of the Bible.

Our society is familiar with the name of Jesus. People hear the name of Jesus and the word *Christian* used many times, but with bewildering and contradictory meanings. In this, our times are similar to those of Jesus himself, when the term *Messiah* was familiar to all, but people could not agree on the meaning of *Messiah*.

Now, as then, the question is not so much, "Do you believe in Jesus?" as it is, "Do you know what you are believing in when you believe in Jesus?"

The letters in this book were written to challenge our society's often distorted ideas of who Jesus is, the too narrow definition of salvation often preached in our churches, the sinful separation of prayer from justice, halfway conversions of our private selves that do not affect our public selves, the forgotten message of Jesus to love our enemies, and the often forgotten vocation of care for God's creation.

The first part of each chapter was originally written as a separate "letter" or pamphlet by John Stoner. To these letters, Lois Barrett has added the parts of each chapter called "Experiencing the Letter" and "Reflecting and Acting."

These letters are written in the hope that the good news about Jesus Christ will be truly good and truly news as it is spoken by American Christians.

Please read these letters carefully and consider whether God is calling you to this understanding of the good news.

In the spirit of God's peace,

John K. Stoner

Lois Barrett

John Stoner and Lois Barrett

Letters to

AMERICAN CHRISTIANS

ONE

Does God Save from Enemies?

Dear Christian Friends in America:

I want to place a question before you. It is this: Does God save people from their enemies?

The question is not as strange as it may sound—if one considers it as a question of faith in God. God is a God of salvation. Therefore, we ask, Does God save from enemies?

Enemies? What Enemies?

"But what is this talk about enemies?" you say. "Christians don't have enemies, do they? They might have trouble getting along with someone at work, a cranky neighbor, or even a spouse on bad days, but enemies? No way."

Oh, yes, that would be nice. But what about . . . let us say . . . the communists. Yes, the communists! Or the terrorists—people who have clearly and forcefully set themselves against you and your way of life. Are these not the enemies of our nation, and therefore our enemies? My question is, Does God save people from enemies like these?

Consider for a moment our situation. The United States budgeted $246 billion in 1985 for national defense against enemies, and billions more in 1986. This was done in spite of the fact that America already has some 13,000 nuclear weapons which can be "delivered" to the Soviet Union. These weapons, we are told, could kill every Russian enemy 20 times over.

This is what we are doing to save ourselves from our enemies. Who is doing it? In the *first* place, the nation is doing it. All of this vast, incomprehensible machinery of death is the result of national policy. Someone has called it "the really gross national product." We could laugh if we did not have to cry. The nation is doing it.

But *second,* you and I are doing this. Our tax dollars are paying for it. If nuclear war ever destroys the world, it will only be because millions of people like you and I gave our consent to the preparations for it. Without our consent it would be impossible.

Third, the church is doing this. That's right, the world teeters on the brink of nuclear holocaust because the church has done its part to push it to the edge. If you doubt this statement, look at the record of the church. Or look at its posture today. Listen especially to the most visible and vocal representatives of the church in America today, the TV preachers. They describe the horrors of communist oppression and then call for more military power to save us from the communists.

To summarize, Americans do have enemies. They are called communists. They may chop wood in Siber-

ia, pick coffee in Central America, or run the bureauc-
racy in China, but whatever they do and wherever
they are, Americans are desperate to defend themselves against them. As a nation we have become willing to gamble the future of the world on our effort to
do so.

Does God Know About This?

Because of this intolerable situation we must ask,
Might God do anything about saving us from our enemies? For an answer, we turn to the Bible, which is
the record of what we know about God's character
and intention.

The Bible shows God as a God of salvation. Psalm
98:1-2 says,

> Sing to the Lord a new song,
>   for he has done marvelous things;
> his right hand and his holy arm
>   have worked salvation for him.
> The Lord has made his salvation known
>   and revealed this righteousness to the nations.

Salvation is the redemption—or liberation—of
people from the power of sin, according to Scripture.
Thus, we are familiar with the church's teaching that
God is both willing and able to save people from the
effects of their sinning. Romans 3:23 says that "all
have sinned and fall short of the glory of God." No
person is exempt from the enslaving and guilt-produc-
ing effects of sin, but salvation is offered to all who
put their trust in God. God frees from the power of
sin and forgives the guilt of sin.

Sin, however, is at work not only in our own lives. It is at work also in the lives of others, causing them to sin against us. The effects of sin in the world are such that all people are not only sinners, but also sinned against. We not only do wrong, but wrong is done to us. In the Bible, the wrong that is done to us by others is called "oppression" and the most common name of those who oppress us is "enemy."

Since God is in the salvation business, is God bringing salvation from all—or only part—of the effects of sin in the world? If the effect of sin is twofold, making all of us both guilty and oppressed, it stands to reason that God's salvation should be twofold, addressing both of these effects of sin.

When we look at Scripture, we find that this is indeed the case. When the children of Israel were suffering oppression under the hand of their national enemy, Egypt, God intervened. The language used to describe his intervention is most instructive. After God delivered the children of Israel at the Red Sea, they sang this song:

> Sing to the Lord,
>   for he is highly exalted.
> The horse and its rider
>   he has hurled into the sea. . . .
> The Lord is my strength and my song;
>   he has become my salvation. . . .
> Your right hand, O Lord,
>   was majestic in power.
> Your right hand, O Lord,
>   shattered the enemy.

> In the greatness of your majesty
>   you threw down those who opposed you.
>
> (Exodus 15)

"The Lord has become my salvation," the Israelites proclaimed after God delivered them from their national enemy.

Most Americans, indeed most Christian Americans, will consider the idea preposterous that God has an interest in saving them from their national enemies. But any careful reading of Scripture reveals that God does in fact save his people from their enemies. A typical expression of this is in Psalm 37:

> The salvation of the righteous comes from the Lord;
>   he is their stronghold in time of trouble.
> The Lord helps them and delivers them;
>   he delivers them from the wicked and saves them,
>   because they take refuge in him.
>
> (Psalm 37:39-40)

So we see God delivering people from oppression, as well as from guilt.

This understanding of God as Savior from both guilt and oppression, from sin and from enemies, is thoroughly biblical, but almost unknown in the churches of America. In the Bible one need look only at the Psalms to see how characteristic is the cry to God for deliverance from enemies and the confession of faith that God will give his deliverance, or salvation. It is an important theme in more than 87 psalms which look to God for deliverance from being sinned against.

The experience of salvation from enemies began to

take a new form in Israel as a new understanding of relationship to enemies was revealed through the prophets during Israel's exile. A spirit of nonretaliation toward oppressors was learned and taught by Isaiah (Isaiah 50 and 52:13—53:12). The book of Jonah challenged Israel to declare to their enemies the message of life through faith in God. Examples of this better way with enemies can be seen in Israel's earlier history as well (e.g., 2 Kings 6:8-23).

In keeping with this emerging understanding, the Gospels portray Jesus as a Savior from powers which oppress, although indeed a Savior who uses unlikely methods and has an unusual form of power. Zechariah prophesied Jesus' birth with this praise to God:

> He has raised up a horn of salvation for us
>   in the house of his servant David
>   (as he said through his holy prophets of long ago),
> salvation from our enemies
>   and from the hand of all who hate us . . .
> to rescue us from the hand of our enemies. . . .
>
> (Luke 1:69-74)

This unusual but vividly specific description of Jesus as Savior from enemies is a bridge between the Testaments. It was fulfilled, according to the apostle Peter, in the ministry of Jesus, who "went around doing good and healing all who were under the power of [oppressed by] the devil, because God was with him" (Acts 10:38).

Those whom Jesus healed were truly saved from their enemies in various ways. First of all, God saved them from the "enemies within" (not only from national or foreign enemies). They were saved from oppressive laws and from the people who made those laws. They were saved from sickness and hunger, and from the people who tolerated and caused sickness and hunger by their pollution and greed.

Second, God saved them from national enemies (the "communists" of their day) in various ways. The book of Acts is the best description of this. To name a few ways God saved them:

1. Avoiding prison sentence (Acts 4:21-22)
2. Release from prison (Acts 5:18-20; 12:1-19; 16:16-40)
3. Suffering but not dying (Acts 5:27-42)
4. Removing the oppressor enemy (Acts 12:1-25)
5. Death without defeat (Acts 7:1-60; 12:1-25)
6. Enemies turned into friends (Acts 9:1-19; 10:1-48; chapters 13—15)

The reader might object that the third and fifth in the list, suffering and dying, are not ways of being saved. But according to Jesus, they are. He said:

> They will put some of you to death.
> All men will hate you because of me.
> But not a hair of your head will perish.
> By standing firm you will gain life.
>
> (Luke 21:16-19)

Jesus does indeed challenge us to rethink our ideas of national security and what it means to be saved. The typical American belief that salvation from enemies must take the form of religious liberty, material prosperity, and escape from suffering is dangerously nearsighted and ultimately ruinous to the human spirit. Jesus is telling us that there is something worth dying for: love, truth, and the kingdom of God. But Jesus never agreed with those who say there is something worth killing for.

If one finds any imbalance from Genesis to Revelation in emphasis on salvation from guilt on the one hand and from oppression on the other, the accent falls on salvation from oppression. God is everywhere called upon to deliver, or save from oppression.

Salvation by Grace

What American Christians face in the twin threats of communism and nuclear war today, is, in fact, a crisis of faith. Will we have faith in God to receive all of the salvation which he offers, or only part of it? Will we limit the biblical witness, confining and restricting salvation by grace, or will we receive the Bible's own testimony, accepting and proclaiming salvation by grace?

There is something very humanistic about the frantic effort to save ourselves from our enemies by military means. It is a denial of grace. Scripture treats it as a denial of God (e.g., Psalm 33, Isaiah 31). When God is not approached in prayer for salvation (from enemies), we deny God. When instead we appeal to human energy, wealth, ingenuity, wisdom, labor, and devices, we are guilty of secular humanism.

We have deadly Titan and Minuteman missiles planted in our soil. We have awesome B52 bombers carrying nuclear warheads across American skies and around the world. We have Trident submarines plying the ocean, each armed with enough nuclear missiles to blow up 408 targets. We have low-altitude Cruise and high-altitude Pershing II missiles dotting the landscape of some Western European countries, and we complain because the Dutch refuse to have these missiles on their soil. Earth, sea, and sky are laced with nuclear bombs, but fear of our enemies drives us to even more bizarre adventures. Outer space is now being targeted for military exploitation, and untold billions of dollars are to be spent on "Star Wars" and "High Frontier."

It is an age-old spiritual struggle in modern dress. Each human era faces its own peculiar crisis of faith. In the time of Jesus it was over Jewish legalism. In the sixteenth century it was over Roman Catholic indulgences and the use of the sword for defense. In our time it is over the idol of militarism. Always there is some human institution, tradition, power, or program offering salvation, if people will only place their trust in it. Humanistic anticommunism has exalted the idol of militarism in our day. The government demands of every citizen a contribution toward the death of the enemy, because it is believed that salvation will come from such human efforts.

The Bible portrays a different understanding of God's will. The psalmist declares, "The Lord is the stronghold [military fortress] of my life—of whom shall I be afraid?" (Psalm 27). The historic peace churches (Brethren, Friends, Mennonites) have believed with the Bible writers that God sees oppression, cares about it, and acts to save its victims (Psalms 9, 10, 11, etc.). This is the grace of God at work. Our confession is that although we can no more save ourselves from our enemies than we can save ourselves from our sins, God offers through Jesus Christ to save us from both.

Experiencing the Letter

Can we really expect God to save us from enemies, even those who threaten to kill us? Sarah Carson and the other Christians in this story did depend on God to save them from armed and hostile soldiers.

Welcoming the Enemy[1]

It was midnight. Before retiring I walked out on the screened porch where my 15-year-old son was sleeping. I was leading a team of 17 young people, including two of my own children, on a three-month work assignment in a jungle area 200 miles from the nearest city in a South American country. Four years before, my husband and I with our four children had first come to this area at the request of the village people to help them start a church, build a fish hatchery, and develop other forms of appropriate technology. After the center had been established we moved to work in another country. This summer the village had asked us to return to experiment with a vegetable protein project.

When we received the invitation, my husband was already committed to a project in Haiti for the sum-

---

[1] By Sarah Carson. Sarah and her husband, Ken, are the founders of SIFAT (Servants in Faith and Technology), which offers practical training in meeting basic human needs. The group is located in Wedowee, Alabama. Reprinted with permission from the April 1983 issue of *Sojourners*, P.O. Box 29272, Washington, DC 20017.

mer. We decided to divide up for three months in order to work in both projects. My husband took our 14-year-old Karen with him to Haiti while our 15-year-old Tommy and 16-year-old Kathy went with me, leaving our 19-year-old Chris to take care of things at our headquarters in Alabama.

The air on the porch was chilly, so I laid a blanket across Tommy's cot, then stood a moment looking out across the fishponds that were bringing hope for more food to our village. The light from the moon made a rippling path of white across the water.

Suddenly I heard a crash. Turning quickly I could see in the moonlight that a soldier had slid into our water barrel. I was paralyzed with shock as I looked out over the clearing that separated our temporary home from the jungle. About 30 soldiers were rushing our house.

Our host country had just held elections, not the usual custom, and the military did not agree with the results. It had taken over one week before, exiling the newly elected president and repressing any resistance, real or imagined. Since we were in such a remote frontier village, I had not expected the fighting to reach us.

While I stood there, frozen in fear, watching the soldiers surround our house, the message a neighbor woman had brought me that day flashed through my mind.

"Sister, keep your team in the house," she had urged. "I just came from the market over near the military camp. I overheard two soldiers saying the Americans were to blame for the resistance." But now what the neighbor woman had warned me about was taking place before my eyes. Evidently, the soldiers were intent on carrying out their threat. If they wanted to kill us, there was no way we could stop them.

My heart was beating so fast, I thought my blood vessels would burst. It felt as if I was about to have a stroke. I knew I had a responsibility for the team members inside the house, but I could not even call out to them. I was paralyzed with fear.

I had only a split second to pray before the soldiers found me: "God, if I have to die, take care of my family. And God, please take away this fear. I don't want to die afraid. Please help me to die trusting you." I was suddenly aware of the presence of God.

We do not always feel God. Usually we trust God by faith. However, at that moment God's presence was very real, seemingly touchable. I still thought I was going to die, but I knew God had things under control. I remember thinking that maybe our deaths would accomplish things that we had not been able to accomplish with our lives.

I found myself stepping up to the closest soldier and speaking words I could never have thought to say. "Welcome, brother," I called out. "Come in. You do not need guns to visit us."

At that the soldier jumped, dropped the bullet he was putting in his gun, and shouted, "Not me. I'm not the one. I'm just following orders. There's the commander over there, he's the one."

I raised my voice and repeated, "You're all welcome. Everyone is welcome in our home."

At that the commander ran up to me, shoved the muzzle of his rifle against my stomach, and pushed me through the door into the house. Thirty soldiers rushed into the house and began pulling everything off the shelves and out of drawers, looking for guns. They herded the team members into the kitchen, where they sat quietly by the glow of the two candles we used for light.

The soldier who led the attack turned his gun on me and demanded angrily, "What are you Americans doing down here—trying to stop our revolution? Seventeen Americans would not be living in this poverty if they did not have political motivation."

"Sir," I responded truthfully, "we have had nothing to do with your revolution. We are here for two reasons. We are teaching self-help projects to the hungry and we are teaching the Bible."

"That tells me nothing," he responded. "I have never read the Bible in my life. Maybe it is a communist book, for all I know."

"You have never read the Bible in your life? Oh, sir, I am so sorry for you. You have missed the best part of your life. Please let me tell you what it says."

He made no objection. He had to stand there with his gun on us while the other soldiers ransacked the house looking for the guns we did not have.

I picked up a Spanish Bible and turned to the Sermon on the Mount. "We teach about Jesus Christ," I said, "God's Son who came into this world to save us. He also taught us a better way than fighting. He taught us the way of love. Because of him I can tell you that even though you kill me, I will die loving you because God loves you. To follow him, I have to love you too."

In that particular Bible there were paragraph captions. He glanced at them and read plainly, "Jesus teaches love your enemies," and "Return good for evil."

"That's humanly impossible!" he burst out.

"That's true, sir," I answered. "It isn't humanly possible, but with God's help it is possible."

"I don't believe it."

"You can prove it, sir. I know you came here to kill us. So just kill me slowly, if you want to prove it. Cut me to pieces little by little, and you will see you cannot make me hate you. I will die praying for you because God loves you, and we love you too."

The soldier lowered his gun and stepped back. Clearing his throat, he said, "You almost convince me you are innocent—but I have orders to take everyone in the house and the ham radio. I will let you get some warm clothes and a blanket—you will be sleeping on the ground."

They marched us two by two at gunpoint down a trail to where a truck was waiting on the one little road that came into our village. We saw that the others in our town had been taken prisoner also. The district superintendent of the church, the leader of the youth group, and other leaders were lined up at gunpoint, ready to be loaded on the trucks with us.

Suddenly the soldier changed his mind: "Halt!" he said. "Take only the men. The women will come with me."

He led us back to our home, saying, "I don't know why I am doing this. I was about to take you into a jungle camp of over a thousand soldiers. I know what they do to women prisoners. You would be abused many times. I cannot take you.

"In our army no one breaks an order," he continued sternly. "I have never broken an order before, but for the first time tonight I am refusing to obey an order. If my superior officer finds out that you were in this house when I raided it, and that I did not take you, I will pay for it with my life." He strode to the door, stopped, and looked back again.

"I could have fought any amount of guns you might have had," he said, "but there is something here I cannot understand. I cannot fight it."

Then the hard part began—waiting to hear what had happened to the men of our team and the leaders of the village. The waiting, the uncertainty, seemed endless. If a twig snapped outside our window everyone jumped, thinking the soldiers were back again. The people of our village were as distressed as we were. They stood around in our house all day—some weeping, others coming to offer their sympathy. No one knew what would happen next.

The local people insisted we could not have a service in the church on Sunday because the soldiers considered any meeting held to be for the purpose of political agitation. "Soldiers will be there if you have a service. They will take more prisoners," they told me. We all agreed to pray at home on Sunday.

But on Saturday night a messenger came to our door. "I bring a message from the man who commanded the attack on your village Thursday night," he said. "He says he will be at your service Sunday. However, he has no vehicle on Sundays so you are to bring the church's jeep and get him. He said to tell you that if you don't come he will be there anyway, even if he has to walk the 10 miles." It sounded like a threat.

I sent a message to everyone in the town that night. "We will have the service after all," I told them, "but you are not obligated to come. In fact you may lose your life by coming. No one knows what this soldier will do. Do not come when the church bell rings unless you are sure God wants you to come." I knew that the villagers feared the military and stayed out of sight when soldiers were around. I did not expect any of them to come.

The next morning I took the jeep and went to get the commander. He came with a bodyguard. The two of them marched coldly into the church and sat down, still holding their rifles. The women on our team came in, the bell was rung, and we began to sing. The church was packed before the first hymn was over. The people came pale and trembling, but they came. They had felt that their faith was at stake, and they were determined to attend, even if it meant imprisonment.

Since the leaders of the church had been taken by the military, I led the service. I tried to do just what I would have done had the soldiers not been there. It was church custom to welcome visitors by inviting them to the platform, singing a welcome song, and waving to them. Everyone would then line up to shake the visitors' hands, hug them, and say some personal words of greeting.

How could I ask these people to hug the very man who had taken their husband, sons, or brother prisoner? That was asking too much. I decided that I would stop there and leave out the hugging.

The soldiers were surprised when I asked them to come to the platform to let us welcome them. "Welcome us?" they asked in amazement. "Well, all right," they shrugged. They came forward and stood very formally with their guns across their backs.

The people stood, singing weakly and waving their hands timidly. I expected them to sit back down, but no. The first man on the front seat came forward and put out his hand. As he bent over to hug the soldier I heard him say, "Brother, we don't like what you did to our village, but this is the house of God, and God loves you, so you are welcome here."

Everyone in the church followed his example, even the women whose eyes were red from weeping for their loved ones whom this man had taken prisoner. They too said words of welcome. The looks on the soldiers' faces became ones of surprise, then incredulity.

When the last person finished greeting them, the head soldier marched to the pulpit and said in a very stern voice, "Now I will have a few words. Never have I ever dreamed that I could raid a town, come back, and have that town welcome me as a brother. I can hardly believe what I have seen and heard this morning. That sister told me Thursday night that Christians love their enemies, but I did not believe her then. You have proven it to me this morning," he said to the congregation.

"This is the first church service I have ever been to," he continued. "I never believed there was a God before, but what I have just felt is so strong that I will never doubt the existence of God again as long as I live."

He turned from one side of the congregation to the other. "Do all of you know God?" he asked. "If you know God, hang on to him. It must be the greatest thing in this world to know God." As he spoke in an urgent voice he motioned with his hand, clenching it as though to hold on to something, while in his other hand he held a gun.

"I don't know God," he confessed in a low voice, "but I hope someday I shall, and that someday we can once again greet each other as brothers and sisters, as we have done this morning."

He came home with us for lunch. The men caught fish from the ponds to cook for his meal. The women helped me cook, even those who had lost a loved one. While we prepared lunch, the men took him around to see the brick project for dry housing, the chicken and vegetable protein project, and the clear water project. At last he said, "I have taken innocent people, but I did not know it when I did it. Now it is too late. If any of you need anything since you do not have your men, please tell me, and I will pay for it out of my pocket." He left, planning a return visit that was never to transpire.

Seven days later the bishop of our church sent a message for all Americans to come immediately to the capital city. He urged us to return to the United States as soon as possible, since he feared that our lives would be endangered by a possible countercoup.

Once in the capital, we learned that the American men who had been taken from our house at midnight had been taken by dump truck to a military camp 10 miles from our village. There they had been loaded on a plane with many other prisoners from the local area and flown to the capital, where they were held in a basement cell.

Three days later the U.S. embassy was successful in negotiating the release of the Americans and helping them leave the country. The local men, however, were not released for two weeks. Some, particularly the religious leaders, were tortured.

Often I think of the soldier and his 30 men who stormed out of the jungle ready to kill us. Within 15 minutes he had changed his mind and risked his life to save us. I thank God for putting divine love in my heart for a person I could not love on my own.

I cannot forget the last thing the soldier said to us as he left: "I have fought many battles and killed many people. It was nothing to me. It was just my job to exterminate them. But I never knew them personally. This is the first time I ever knew my enemy face to face, and I believe that if we knew each other, our guns would not be necessary."

Reflecting and Acting

Who are your enemies? Who are the people who have hurt you or threatened to hurt you? Who are the people with whom you are uncomfortable? Make a list.

What have you done to save yourself from your enemies?

What have you asked other people to do?

Do you feel you were following the way of Jesus in what you did? Did you confront your enemies with love? Did you run away in fear? Or did you try to fight fire with fire?

Often when we try to fight back on the enemy's own terms, we become like the enemy. We also become oppressors when we counteract violent oppression with more violence. We have let the enemy's action control our actions. We are no longer free. We are no longer listening to God's Spirit.

When we depend on God to save us from our enemies, we depend on God's Spirit to tell us what to do. Even if the enemies are violent, we do not let their violence be contagious. We counter hatred with love. We reject both fight and flight. We let God's love shine through us. And we expect the grace of God's salvation both for ourselves and our enemies. We ask God to lead us on a level path, not affected by the actions of our enemies (see Ps. 27:11).

Pray. To help you pray to God for salvation from your enemies, use Psalm 27 as a model. Where the psalm mentions enemies, adversaries, foes, false witnesses, etc., substitute the names of individuals or nations which you included on your list of enemies above.

When we trust in God and are not afraid of our enemies, then we can dwell in God's house all the days of our lives and see the beauty of God's salvation.

TWO

A Disarming Initiative by Jesus

Dear Christian Friends in America:

If God had not been willing to take the first step of unilateral disarmament, you would never have heard of Jesus Christ. But God did come into his world—a world bristling with enemies and hostility—as a disarmed child. He lived a life of resistance to the powers of death and endured suffering. He did not retaliate against his enemies who pursued him to the cross. Then he rose from the dead to justify this unusual way of life.

The story of Jesus Christ places an event of unilateral disarmament at the center of world history. The time is right for the church in the United States to proclaim the meaning of this transforming, disarming initiative for our world which is being consumed by a deadly arms race.

The nuclear arms race may be the most urgent threat ever to face the human race. If it is that, or anything close to it, then Christian people must be expected to say what their faith has to offer a desperate world. My message is that what God did in Jesus Christ speaks to our situation.

The Communist Threat

The nuclear arms race has become what it is because of fear. If you, like most Americans, are afraid of what the enemies of America could do, you might not be paranoid. Paranoia is irrational fear of imaginary enemies. Genuine fear is apprehension based on a reasonable evaluation of the situation.

We Americans are brought up on stories of communist atrocities. From the time we were children on our mother's laps we heard of the persecution of Christians, jailing of innocent people, and execution of "enemies of the state" by the communists. In school the *Weekly Reader* carried stories of communist aggression, the red plague spreading over the earth like a giant blood stain. On TV the communists are the bad guys, heartless revolutionaries, or scheming spies. It is a great mixture of fact and fiction, but it all combines to instill deep and persistent fear. And if all the fiction were removed, enough fact would remain to justify a real sober fear.

So, out of all of these fears are born thoughts of how to protect ourselves from our enemies. The individual looks to the nation for defense. The nation uses force and the power of death as the way to deal with enemies. And so the military engine is started and the wheels begin to turn.

As old as Cain and as new as the bomber pilot just out of flight school, death is our choice. Our society becomes obsessed with death. The TV portrays killing as the solution for everything from treason, to robbery, to rape, to insult. Life is cheap. And so the instruments of death must be available and cheap. We become a gun culture.

But guns are too small and bullets too limited for global fears of foreign enemies. So bombs are invented. But "conventional" bombs are too small. So again the engine whirs as the wheels turn in pursuit of a bigger and better bomb. Perhaps, could it be, somewhere locked up in the secrets of the universe, is the Ultimate Weapon, the biggest bomb of all?

August 6, 1945—it falls on Hiroshima
August 9, 1945—it falls on Nagasaki

So now we have it. But it also has us. And now the soul of our nation has been wounded and all but destroyed by the bombs which hold our enemies hostage. Our gun held at their head is wired to their gun held at our head, and deep within both of us the soul is dying. We have become willing to do worse to them—guilty and innocent together—than they have threatened to do to us. We are beginning to doubt that we are much better than they.

To sum up, in the real world there are enemies which cause genuine fear. But the attempt to deal with enemies by the power of death has brought the world to the brink of global suicide and has nearly destroyed the soul of our nation. Is there no other way? Must everyone embrace the powers of death until the world consumes itself in a vast orgy of killing? Does everyone have to support the nuclear solution?

God's Bold Disarming Initiative in Christ

If we can believe what God did in Jesus Christ, the answer is "no." There is another way of dealing with enemies, and we have seen it. Moreover, we have seen it not as a theory in a book or an idea somewhere else, but as an invasion of our world and a transformation of our lives. It is a story entrusted to the church in the Bible. But the church has often obscured, misunderstood, and ignored the other way of dealing with enemies. Here is the story.

When Jesus Christ was about to be born, a wise man named Zechariah prophesied in these words:

> Praise be to the Lord, the God of Israel,
>   because he has come and has redeemed his people.
> He has raised up a horn of salvation for us
>   in the house of his servant David . . .
> salvation from our enemies
>   and from the hand of all who hate us.
>
> (Luke 1:68-71)

This promise of salvation from enemies was fulfilled in unexpected ways. The people who understood and received this salvation in Jesus' time were few, and relatively few receive it today. But the possibility of receiving it is open to all. The church of Jesus Christ should lead the way.

Look at what Jesus did. He came to enemies. That is, he lived in this world—what "realists" (peace through strength people) like to call "the real world"— and he faced life-threatening enemies.

Who were the enemies of Jesus? Did he have enemies? The answer is in two parts. First, as the incarnation of God, Jesus was opposed in some way by every person who in some way opposed good. That included everyone. So, in that sense, Jesus saw everyone as an enemy (all have sinned and rebelled against God). Everyone needed to be responded to as one responds to an enemy.

Second, Jesus faced people who opposed him (made themselves his enemies) by specific, hostile actions intended ultimately to kill him. The scribes and the Pharisees, representatives of the Jewish religious power structure, and Herod and the Roman authorities are identified in Scripture as life-threatening enemies of Jesus. For Jesus' fellow Jews, the Romans were the communists of the day, a foreign military power depriving their nation of its freedom. It is therefore useful in understanding the life and ministry of Jesus to say that he faced a "communist threat" like the one we face today.

So Jesus had to respond to enemies, just as we do. The question is, What kind of response to enemies did he make? Was it the power of death response which has been used by people and nations from Cain to twentieth-century nuclear deterrence? How did Jesus respond to enemies whose method was military and whose power was death? Can we look in a fresh way at the story of Jesus, and see it taking place in a real world like our own? Can we see Jesus having to make hard choices, tough choices because he carried responsibility for the defense of his people, as their leader sent by God? Let's go back to the source and let the Gospel writer Luke tell us about Jesus.

The Teaching of Jesus

When Jesus came on the scene in ancient Palestine he caused quite a stir. Luke reports the prophecies of Mary and Zechariah, angel appearances, the controversial figure of John the Baptist, including his imprisonment by Herod, the baptism of Jesus, his temptation, and his rejection in the synagogue at Nazareth. Luke shows his growing fame as a healer of lepers, the blind, and the demon-possessed. He reports the growing controversy with Jewish authorities over laws of Sabbath and fasting. After observing all of this, people were certainly wondering what the message of Jesus was. What did Jesus have to say? What did he expect people to do? The readers of Luke's Gospel naturally wonder, What does this Teacher teach?

But Luke makes his readers wait until the sixth chapter before he gives the teaching of Jesus. Like a skillful writer, he lays the background in chapters 1 through 5, creating expectation, building suspense. Those chapters present no sermon by Jesus, no summary of his message, no commands to all the people which would put him in the tradition of Moses, God's appointed lawgiver.

But in chapter 6 Luke lifts the cover. He shows Jesus asserting his authority as Lord of even the Sabbath by gathering grain and healing on the Sabbath. He shows him establishing his role as leader of nothing less than a new Israel by appointing twelve apostles. Then the stage is set for his teaching. A large crowd of his disciples and people from all over the region gather on a level place, and Jesus stands before them and speaks:

> Blessed are you who are poor,
> for yours is the kingdom of God.
> Blessed are you who hunger now . . .
>
> (Luke 6:20-21)

and so forth. Jesus speaks to them descriptively at
first, telling them what the facts of life are—how life
really works in God's plan and time. Still there is no
command, no demand, no imperative.

But then comes the first word of command from the
lips of Jesus, who is the Son of God and Son of man,
the Word made flesh, God in human form, the hope
of the ages, the way, the truth, and the life. Listen to
him:

> But I tell you who hear me: Love your enemies, do
> good to those who hate you, bless those who curse
> you, pray for those who mistreat you. If someone
> strikes you on one cheek, turn to him the other also.
> If someone takes your cloak, do not stop him from
> taking your tunic. Give to everyone who asks you,
> and if anyone takes what belongs to you, do not
> demand it back. Do to others as you would have them
> do to you. (Luke 6:27-31)

"Love your enemies." Those are the first words
which Jesus spoke as a general command to the
people on this earth. They sound like words from
another planet, or another realm, because the human
family has not been responding to its enemies with
love. The human (or humanistic) way has been to
respond to enemies with the power of death.

But Jesus does not stop with the paragraph we have

quoted. He has more to say to enforce the point, to make it plain, inescapable, awesome, and unavoidable. Listen:

> If you love those who love you, what credit is that to you? Even "sinners" love those who love them. And if you do good to those who are good to you, what credit is that to you? Even "sinners" do that. And if you lend to those from whom you expect repayment, what credit is that to you? Even "sinners" lend to "sinners," expecting to be repaid in full. But love your enemies, do good to them, and lend to them without expecting to get anything back. Then your reward will be great, and you will be sons of the Most High, because he is kind to the ungrateful and wicked. Be merciful, just as your Father is merciful.
>
> (Luke 6:32-36)

Only one imperative is repeated in this paragraph: "Love your enemies."

We live in a time when Christians will take almost anyone's word more seriously than that of Jesus. On the question of how to respond to enemies, they will listen to a politician, a barber, a psychologist, a dog catcher, or nuclear physicist—almost anyone—before they will listen to Jesus. That is why we have quoted his words at such length.

Luke confronts us with the fact that the central element of the call to conversion by Jesus was the command to love enemies. No other prophet or teacher in all of history had ever been so bold as to make the love of enemies his most important teaching. In John's Gospel the centrality of love is emphasized by calling it a new (eleventh!) commandment (13:34). Clearly, Jesus calls people to something which they cannot do by their own strength. But that is what conversion is about! It is to make people what they were not before, to make possible what was not possible before.

The Life of Jesus

So the words of Jesus are clear. But what about his life? Did he do what he commanded others to do? When we look at what Jesus did, we find that his actions speak louder than his words.

Jesus lived a disarmed life. His disarmament was, moreover, unilateral in the most precise sense of the term. His enemies had not disarmed themselves, nor had they made any promise to do so. That is why we have called his action a bold, disarming initiative, with astonishing impact on world events.

The obedience of the Son to the Father's will that he should love his enemies was crucial. All who would be followers of Jesus are called to that same obedience. Jesus did good to those who hated him, he blessed those who cursed him, and he prayed for those who mistreated him. These are actions which can be called "transforming initiatives," to use the phrase of Glen Stassen. They are enemy-loving actions with potential for changing the course of history.

But Jesus not only loved his enemies. He also challenged and resisted the evil that was at work in them. Indeed, it was this resistance to evil which often led Jesus into conflict with people. The resistance of Jesus was directed toward those spiritual powers of evil and death which impinge on persons. Jesus was nonresistant toward the persons themselves.

This is illustrated in the way Jesus raised the issue of the Sabbath law with the Pharisees. Jesus exposed an injustice, made a public issue of it, and as a consequence stirred up trouble. He exposed the enslaving power of the law over the lives of the Pharisees. This was beneficial to the Pharisees as oppressors, by helping them to see their situation and repent if they chose to. It was also beneficial to the sick (the oppressed) for obvious reasons. Thus, by resisting the powers of death, Jesus placed himself on the side of the oppressed, showed clearly that he did not pamper oppressors. He took upon himself the blows of oppressors, which led him ultimately to the cross.

But the resurrection followed the cross because God was involved in the process. The letter to the Philippians says of Jesus:

> He humbled himself
> and became obedient to death—
>   even death on a cross!
> Therefore God exalted him to the highest place.
>   (Philippians 2:8-9)

God was pleased with the obedience of Jesus to the way of humility, the way of enemy love. Therefore God exalted him, raising him from the dead. This was God's way of showing that the way of loving enemies is the right way. It was God's way of saving Jesus from his enemies. And it is our reason for saying that the way of unilateral disarmament works.

Jesus loved his enemies and they killed him. The same thing may happen to us. Are we ready for that? Would we choose to follow Jesus if we knew that it meant that? This is not a new question. It is the old question, the original question which all the people around Jesus and his disciples faced. We see them struggling with it as they gradually begin to understand that Jesus is a suffering Messiah who loves his enemies, not a military messiah who kills them.

In Mark 8:1—9:13, as the true identity of Jesus as a suffering, enemy-loving Messiah begins to emerge, we see the blindness as well as the beginning sight of the disciples. Jesus says that anyone who would come after him must deny himself and take up his cross (that is, accept suffering and even death). Jesus warns that if anyone is ashamed of him and his words, the Son of man will be ashamed of him.

How ironic and instructive that later Peter would be the one who would be ashamed of this pacifist Jesus and his words about loving enemies! Unable to bear identification with such a man, Peter denies that he knows him (Mark 14:27-72). This is the Peter who did not accept the discipline and power of prayer when the crisis of enemy action was upon Jesus and his small band, but relied instead on the sword (Mark 12:43-52). But Peter changed after the resurrection because the resurrection changed everything.

It may be objected that the life and teaching of Jesus are the standard for personal ethics but not for social ethics. It has often been said that there is a difference between the way a person should respond to individual enemies and the way a group should respond to national enemies. The failure of this interpretation is that it confines Jesus to a preconceived box—an individualistic box which wrenches Jesus out of his historical role as a national leader.

The traditional distinction between personal and social ethics can make Jesus irrelevant to national policy only if it is possible to have a king with no subjects, a priest with no worshipers, a prophet with no audience, a kingdom with no power, a triumphal entry with no public emotion, a crucifixion of an altogether virtuous man with no public objection, and a resurrection with no political impact. Jesus was a public figure, as the foregoing list demonstrates. He was a national leader and he acted deliberately as such. If Jesus was a private figure, whose teaching and actions are relevant only for private application, he was this in the same way that Karl Marx and George Washington were private figures.

We have seen that the teaching and the life of Jesus unite with awesome consistency in their command to love enemies and accept suffering. We may find this overwhelming. We also find it plain beyond dispute. The command makes sense only when linked with the resurrection.

The centrality of the resurrection for discussions of pacifism and international relations is denied by humanists because they do not believe in a resurrection, and by many Christians because they declare the resurrection irrelevant to this discussion. The effect of both is the same. The Bible, in contrast, asserts that the resurrection of Jesus Christ is of decisive relevance, even as his cross—his unilaterally disarmed expression of enemy love—is relevant to the arms race and the fate of the earth.

Experiencing the Letter
The following is the experience of Kathy Royer, Elk-

hart, Indiana, as she struggled with her response to nuclear weapons:[1]

The window just to my right reflected the images of the faces of those who were gathered in the Holy Rosary Catholic Church in Glenwood, Iowa. The reflections of those who were gathered to think and pray together about the sinful use of nuclear weapons were superimposed on a group of local church members who were gathered behind that window in a small prayer chapel to pray for peace.

I was part of the large group of approximately 500 who had come together from all over the United States. We are a great variety of people. Some of us were active in social justice concerns in the communities in which we lived. We were a vital group. We were an action-oriented group. We sang, prayed, and discussed. We were passionate and serious and boisterous as we pondered the possibility of moving outside the law to communicate our concern about the proliferation of machines of death and destruction to those in power at the Strategic Air Command just twenty miles away.

We were together for two days from early morning until late at night and all the while the silent vigil of prayer continues in the small chapel. We could see young men and women—some of them obviously teenagers—come and go. We watched during the day as older people—possibly retired—knelt. Sometimes working men would come and kneel still dressed in

[1]The following is reprinted from *Peace Section Newsletter*, May-June 1985 (15:3), pp. 1, 12.

their khaki work clothes. Other times there were young mothers. I didn't talk to the people who were praying but their presence gave me an energy and a power in a way that I had not experienced before.

I came to the retreat from a life that had taught me that Jesus is the answer. Because of the strong faith of my parents, I learned that Christianity makes a difference in every part of life. As I grew, I became aware that sin was rampant in the world. I saw with my own eyes the raw violence of life in southern Africa. I came to the conclusion that if Jesus is the answer then he must be in the midst of the terrible sin of the world. I understood from what I had learned about Jesus that it was his followers who were responsible to be his messengers in the world. To me the message became clear: If Jesus is the answer, then I am called to be the messenger. This was a most frightening conclusion. I was scared when I went to Iowa.

As I sat in that church for those two days, I thought of many reasons why I could not or should not take Jesus' message to the people who were making and planning war at the Strategic Air Command. I thought of my two children back in Indiana—what jeopardy would they be in if I took the risk of carrying Jesus' message? I thought of my job and my husband and all that we were working for in Indiana. My travel plans loomed before me—could I rearrange my schedule to include the many possibilities that breaking the law presented? I thought about the fact that my action would never change the minds of those in power in our military system. I knew in that way it would be futile.

Every now and then as I pondered these questions I

would glance through the window at my right and I would see those people praying for peace. I would feel the power of their prayers and I would know that I was part of that prayer. They were doing their part. Could I do mine? Just as my face was reflected on the glass through which I could see the people in prayer, so also were we connected to one another—those prayers and I. I felt the strength of their silent vigil, and I knew that I could offer myself to be at least part of the way in which their prayers could be embodied in action. I knew that their prayers without real live, flesh-and-blood people to carry the message of Jesus to the world would be empty. I also knew that my action without the power of the Spirit of God would be weak.

On the last night of the retreat, I decided. I would go with those who were going to try to speak to the generals who planned the strategies of war. I knew that I would be breaking the law because the generals did not want to talk with us. I also knew that I was empowered by my prayers and the prayers of those around me. I knew that the message of the gospel needed to be carried into the midst of the sinful world. I was ready.

The next morning as we met for worship we could still see, through our reflection in the windows, the people gathered to pray in the small chapel. My eyes moved from the cross that hung before us to my reflection in the chapel window and then beyond to the people kneeling in prayer. I joined my voice with those around me as we sang a song that summed up my feelings, "Here I am, Lord. Is it I, Lord? I have heard you calling in the night. I will go, Lord, if you lead me. I will hold your people in my heart."

Reflecting and Acting

Politics in the Gospel of Luke. In our time, the heresy of many churches is to treat Jesus' cross and resurrection as irrelevant to part of life—in particular to social ethics. They have been taught not to notice how political are the Gospels.

Study the first six chapters of the Gospel of Luke and list all the political words and ideas that you find there.

Here is a sample:

> *Jesus* (Luke 1:31). The name itself means "savior, deliverer, liberator." It is the Greek form of the Hebrew name, *Joshua.*

> *Throne* and *reign* (Luke 1:32-33). The promise of the angel Gabriel to Mary is that Jesus will be a king.

> "He has put down the mighty from their thrones, and exalted those of low degree" (Luke 1:52). This verse and the rest of Mary's Song of Praise are downright revolutionary.

> *Lord* (Luke 2:11). The Romans called Caesar "Lord." The Jews called God as King "Lord."

> *Salvation* (Luke 2:30). This word was applied not only to the personal realm or to the soul, but to the political realm. The deliverance of a nation from its enemies was also salvation.

"You are my son" (Luke 3:22). This message is also found in Psalm 2:7. There, God's Son is the King of Zion!

"And the devil took him up, and showed him all the kingdoms of the world. . . ." (Luke 4:5). One of the temptations was for Jesus to be a king using the devil's kind of authority. Jesus does not reject kingship, but rejects the worship and service of the devil.

Gospel or *good news* (Luke 4:18). This is not just any old good news. This Greek word was used for the message which the herald of the king brought.

Kingdom (Luke 4:43, etc.). *Kingdom* is a supremely political word. We are so used to reading it metaphorically in the Gospels that we forget about its primary meaning.

Tax collectors (Luke 5:29). Tax collectors were Jews to whom Romans had given a franchise to collect taxes for the government. They were considered traitors and collaborators by faithful Jews. Jesus ate and drank with tax collectors.

Zealots (Luke 6:15). At least one of Jesus' disciples, possibly more, were Zealots. These were members of an informal revolutionary political party who wanted to be rid of Roman rule, even if it meant armed revolt.

This is the setting of Jesus' Sermon on the Plain, with its command to "love your enemies." What enemies do you think Jesus and his hearers had in mind?
Read Jesus' "inaugural address" (Luke 4:16-30).

Who would have been happy to hear him? Which people were upset?

Cross and resurrection. Why does the command to love enemies make sense only when linked with the resurrection?

If you were suffering because of your love for enemies and had no hope in a resurrection, how would you feel about continuing to love your enemies? Would you feel that God was just?

The cross was not only something that Jesus did for us; the cross is also something we are called to take up. The cross is not just any illness or hardship or consequence of our own misdeeds. The cross means suffering at the hands of enemies without using violence against them, with forgiveness toward them, with love toward enemies.

Likewise, the resurrection is not just something God did for Jesus. The fifteenth chapter of 1 Corinthians argues that, like Christ, we too shall be raised from the dead. Christ's resurrection is, in fact, just the "first-fruits of those who have fallen asleep" (v. 20). Because God has raised Christ, God will raise us also.

In the final victory, wrote the apostle Paul, Christ's kingdom will win out over every other authority and power. The resurrection of all the saints is the final blow to all governments and authorities that try to rule with the power of death.

The kind of government that can be run on a platform of enemy-love is a government that operates on the power of the resurrection.

THREE

Social Justice and Spirit Renewal

Dear Christian Friends in America:

The winds of spiritual renewal are blowing across the world. The emergence of spiritual growth groups, the charismatic renewal, and Protestant interest in Catholic spirituality are signs of it. At the same time, the lives of many Christians are marked by spiritual dryness and a gnawing hunger to go deeper into the Spirit of God.

Also across the world, the winds of revolution are blowing. They are rising from the cry of the poor and the oppressed in whom the spirit of life is almost crushed. In Central America, Africa, Asia, and in the cities and mountains of America, the cry for relief from oppression is heard.

The church in America, meanwhile, seems to be divided between those who are pursuing spiritual renewal and those who are pursuing social justice. Where is all of this taking us?

The Cry of the Oppressed

We may be better acquainted with the cry of the heart for spiritual renewal than with the cry of the oppressed for social justice, so I will speak more of the latter in these introductory paragraphs. We know more of the cry for spiritual renewal simply because we live with our own spiritual needs. And we read magazines and watch TV programs which speak more of spiritual needs and renewal than of oppression. But the cry of the oppressed comes to the ears of God and we must allow it to come to our ears.

> Then the Lord said, "I have seen the *affliction* of my people who are in Egypt, and have heard their cry because of their taskmasters."
>
> (Exodus 3:7, RSV)

God says, "I have seen and I have heard," and you and I must take note. God did not stop seeing and responding to oppression 3,000 years ago. What God did then, he is doing now.

A seminary student, who wanted to see how much interest God had in the poor and the oppressed, decided to cut out of the Bible every verse dealing with the poor or economic justice. When he was finished cutting, the Bible that remained wouldn't hold together! A friend said to him, "This is the American Bible today."

Oppression is a common concept in the Bible. What is oppression? It is sin working in one person's life to the hurt of another person. Various words convey the idea of oppression in Scripture.

Again I looked and saw all the *oppression* that
was taking place under the sun:
  I saw the tears of the *oppressed*—
  and they have no comforter;
  power was on the side of their *oppressors*—
  and they have no comforter.

(Ecclesiastes 4:1)

The people of the land practice extortion and commit
robbery; they *oppress* the poor and needy and *mistreat*
the alien, denying them justice.

(Ezekiel 22:29)

Woe to those who make unjust laws,
  to those who issue *oppressive* decrees,
to deprive the poor of their rights
  and withold justice form the *oppressed* of my people,
making widows their prey
  and robbing the fatherless.

(Isaiah 10:1-2)

Why are poor people poor? In the Bible the most
common explanation is oppression. The powerful use
their power to deny justice to the poor (as in the
verses above). The Christians of America are, for the
most part, among the rich and the powerful of the
world. Certainly our nation is the richest and most
powerful nation of the world.

In this situation a critical question for American
Christians is this: Are powerful corporations and
political policies in the United States oppressing the
poor of America's cities and small farms and the poor
of other nations such as Brazil, El Salvador, South

Africa, and the Philippines? The poor who live in those places say they are oppressed by America. Have we heard their cry? Have we given ourselves a chance to hear their cry or have we closed our eyes to every face except those on the TV, and our ears to every voice except those that say what we want to hear? There are study tours to third world countries to help us meet the poor. There are news and discipleship magazines like *Sojourners* and *The Other Side* which let the poor speak for themselves. Are we able to hear? Willing to hear?

Perhaps we try to quiet our bad conscience for neglect of the poor by something we call social concern. But the Bible knows nothing of social concern. The word "social" is not in the Bible and neither is the word "concern" (with this meaning). What is in the Bible, however, is the word *justice,* meaning right, claim, or due.

Justice in the Bible refers to what belongs to persons because of their rights as persons made in the image of God. So when the poor are denied justice (as in the "oppression" verses quoted above), it means they are denied the land, the food, the clothing, and the work which is theirs by right as human beings. To do justice in Scripture means to see to it that poor, weak, or socially outcast persons receive what is theirs by right.

Moreover, to do justice in the biblical sense is spiritual work of the first order. God is intensely, passionately, and eternally interested in seeing that justice is done. He wants to see oppression made right. Jesus called blessed those who hunger and thirst to see right prevail. To do justice is pleasing to God. We see in this a coming together of spiritual renewal and social justice. This unity of spirituality and justice is rooted in the Holy Spirit of God, the third person of the Trinity.

The Mission of the Holy Spirit in Our World

The Holy Spirit is the creating, life-giving, justice-making, peacemaking, and redeeming (or re-creating) Spirit according to Scripture. The Bible shows God creating by the Spirit: "The Spirit of God was hovering over the waters. And God said, 'Let there be light,' and there was light" (Gen. 1:2-3). The psalmist rejoices in God's living creatures:

> How many are your works, O Lord!
>   In wisdom you made them all;
>   the earth is full of your creatures. . . .
> When you send your Spirit,
>   they are created,
>   and you renew the face of the earth.
>
> (Psalm 104:24, 30)

The Spirit is wind, or breath. God has breathed the breath of life into every living creature through his life-giving Spirit.

But the Spirit does not only create and breathe in life. The Spirit also establishes justice when life has gone awry, when oppression has come into the relationships of God's image-bearing children, when the world languishes under monstrous acts of injustice, cruelty, deprivation, greed, deception, torture, violence, atrocity, persecution, killing, and holocaust. Who can measure the suffering that happens every day on the face of the earth, from the streets of the South Bronx to the sunbaked hillsides and dark prisons of El Salvador because of evil at work in the hearts of people—because of the absence of God's Spirit in the human spirit?

Isaiah, looking out upon a world as evil and bent on destruction as our own (lacking only the technology to administer death on a twentieth-century scale), was inspired by God to speak of the coming ministry of the Holy Spirit:

> For the palace will be forsaken,
>   the populous city deserted;
> the hill and the watchtower
>   will become dens for ever,
>   a joy of wild asses,
>   a pasture of flocks;
> until the Spirit is poured upon us from on high,
> and the wilderness becomes a fruitful field
> and the fruitful field is deemed a forest.
> Then justice will dwell in the wilderness,
>   and righteousness abide in the fruitful field.
> And the effect of righteousness will be peace,
>   and the result of righteousness, quietness and trust
> for ever.
>
> (Isaiah 32:14-17, RSV)

Here we are plainly told that justice and peace are the result of the Spirit's outpouring.

In chapter 42 Isaiah links the outpouring of the Spirit with the coming of God's chosen servant (Jesus):

Behold my servant . . . in whom my soul delights;
I have put my Spirit upon him,
  he will bring forth justice to the nations. . . .
  He will faithfully bring forth justice.

(42:1-3, RSV)

The reader will remember that when Jesus began his public ministry in the synagogue at Nazareth, he read these words from Scripture:

The Spirit of the Lord is upon me,
because he has anointed me to
  preach good news to the poor . . .
to set at liberty those who are oppressed.

(Luke 4:18, RSV)

Here, in his inaugural address, Jesus says that his spirituality will be expressed in his special ministry to the poor, the oppressed, the captives, and the blind.

That Spirit-filled people are to follow Jesus in doing these ministries is confirmed after Pentecost, when in the book of Acts the disciples feed the poor, lift the oppressed, release the captives, give sight to the blind, and proclaim the year of the Lord's liberation to the courts and kings of the established oppressors.

Our Spirituality in the Twentieth Century

How then shall we live if this Holy Spirit has filled and taken control of our lives? Our lives should look like Jesus' life if we—like he—are filled with the Holy Spirit. Jesus said, "As the Father has sent me, I am sending you. . . . Receive the Holy Spirit" (John 20:21-22). We know that Jesus was sent disarmed into a

world of enemies, toward whom he showed transforming initiatives of love. Jesus resisted evil (the
powers of death) and exposed sin, especially the sins
of oppressors. By this he hoped to lead oppressors to
repentance and bring justice to the oppressed. We,
too, are called to this kind of life.

A burning passion to see justice done has caused
many people to adopt the methods of force and
violence to deal with oppressors. This is evident on
both the left and right of the political spectrum. To
the left, the cry for liberation of the poor has led
many to accept revolutionary violence. To the right,
fear of communist oppression and outrage at denial of
freedom has led most Americans to accept counter-
revolutionary violence, of which the nuclear arms race
is the most costly and horrendous example. Both sides
of the political spectrum call on the other to renounce
violence, but they will not do so themselves. Both
have adopted the same method: violence. They have
the same goal: to destroy their enemies.

In this situation, a truly Christian alternative of
spiritual power is available. But to release this power,
Christians will have to care deeply about spirituality.
Prayer is the basic form of spiritual expression. Our
passion for justice will have to be linked with prayer
as it was in the life of Jesus.

Our spirituality will show itself in prayer for our
enemies. Jesus is the example of this in the garden of
Gethsemane, praying for his enemies who approached
to arrest him while his disciples slept. The Spirit of
God indwelling Jesus led him to prayer. Prayer was
the defense which Jesus cast up against his enemies. It
was his national security, his tanks, planes, sub-

marines, and nukes. I have written in the second letter ("A Disarming Initiative by Jesus") how Jesus called his disciples to do the same thing and how it all came out in the end for Jesus.

Unfortunately, many Christians have not given much thought to the relationship between prayer and oppression, or prayer and enemies. Their spirituality is compartmentalized away from the real world where people experience injustice, oppression, and threats from living, breathing enemies. So let us consider prayer as a response to enemies who inflict oppression, whether from the political right or the political left. Prayer is effective in six ways.

1. *Prayer enables us to see the enemy in a different way.* Prayer will sometimes show us that we were mistaken about the enemy's intentions, methods, or identity. In every conflict situation, the possibilities for mistaking the issues are immense. We have all experienced this when we were in the third party role. We may have observed a marital conflict between two persons who happened to be our friends. They may have seen each other as oppressors, or enemies. But we could see ways in which they were confusing the issues. Prayer quiets us and allows God to say some things to us which we could never hear otherwise above the noise of our emotions.

2. *Prayer clarifies our thinking about what we are trying to protect or obtain from our enemies.* Should everything which the military system aims to defend in fact be defended? What things do Americans want to defend from their enemies? For example, are Americans trying to defend their access to the wealth of nations around the world so that they can have two cars, split-

level homes, steak, and cake? The danger of going to war to maintain a system of economic injustice is immensely greater than most people think. And on the other hand, oppressed people should stop to ask whether what they really want can be wrested from their oppressors by the powers of death.

3. *Prayer allows God to show us alternative courses of action which we had not thought of before.* Johannes Hamel, a pastor in communist East Germany, speaks of God "making room" or "opening doors" as the believer walks obediently a step at a time. In his book *How to Serve God in a Marxist Land* he writes:

> Time and again God creates loopholes, so to speak, open space in the midst of closed systems of unbelief and hatred of God. Here the possibility is offered and realized for doing the good, reasonable and well-pleasing, although these systems theoretically seem to leave no room for such action.

This is quoted by John Howard Yoder in his book, *What Would You Do?* (Herald Press, 1983). Yoder's book gives many creative suggestions on responding to enemies.

4. *Prayer opens us and the situation to God's intervention with power far superior to that of the enemy.* Prayer is thus the one clear check against humanism, because it specifically invites and waits on God's action in the situation. Many times throughout history God's people have been physically saved from the intention of enemies to kill them through the intervention of God's power. This is not a guaranteed result but it has happened too often to be dismissed as an impossibil-

ity. But violent response does not guarantee the physical safety of those who are threatened, either. The use of force and the use of prayer are both risky. In the Christian understanding of how the world works, prayer releases more power to save innocent people from oppression than do armies and bombs. Prayer opens the channel for God to save us from our enemies. We have written on this subject in the first letter ("Does God Save from Enemies?").

5. *Prayer reminds us that Christ died for the people who are our enemies.* It is helpful to stop and think that anything we contemplate doing to our enemies, we are doing to people for whom Jesus Christ suffered the agonies of the cross. The cross is the irrefutable sign of God's love for enemies. That is the nature of the God we serve. Does the world see that in the message and behavior of the church? Jesus said, "If you want to be children of your heavenly Father, love your enemies." Jim Wallis wrote in his book *The Call to Conversion:* "Fervent prayer for our enemies is a great obstacle to war and the feelings that lead to it."

6. *Prayer brings us into the presence of God, which is finally what salvation means.* To be strengthened for life, to rise above the effects of sin in our own lives and the oppression we face because of sin in the lives of others, we need to know God. Prayer is opening ourselves to the presence of God.

The first Christians, whose story is told in the book of Acts, faced enemies as determined and cruel as any we know. How did they respond? Prayer was the heart of their response. A careful reading of Acts shows that prayer in the face of enemy threats had the kind of effects we have been describing here.

Prayer, however, did not always save their lives. Jesus had spoken to them about enemies with these words:

> They will put some of you to death. All men will hate you because of me. But not a hair of your head will perish. By standing firm you will gain life.
>
> (Luke 21:16-19)

Here in a single breath Jesus says that some of you will be put to death, not a hair of your head will perish, and you will save yourselves. Can you die and be saved at the same time?

Stephen's martyrdom explains this, as much as it can be explained. In the story we see Stephen surrounded by enemies. They are making false accusations against him. His response is not to call the church to arms against the apostate Jewish leadership or to demand a Roman legion to guarantee his religious freedom (which was certainly being threatened). Rather, Stephen spoke the Word of God with boldness, telling all that God had done to save people from their sins and their enemies.

When the crowd pressed harder, he knelt and prayed.

Then he looked up to heaven and saw the glory of God and Jesus standing on the right hand of God. In that moment of supreme crisis, God was revealed to Stephen. That is how God saved Stephen from his enemies. The revelation of God through Jesus Christ is salvation. Stephen died with a prayer of forgiveness on his lips. And so he was saved from his enemies.

Who can say how many innocent lives were saved

from death that day and in the days that followed because Stephen gave his life for his people and for Christ?

Here is spiritual power at work in the world, establishing justice and making peace, as Isaiah said the Holy Spirit would do when poured out on the earth. Let us seek the spiritual renewal which this understanding of the Holy Spirit, prayer, justice, love, and power can release in our midst.

Experiencing the Letter[1]

David Hayden is a Mennonite minister in Roanoke, Virginia. In the following interview with Biff Weidman, David offers a glimpse of life at Justice House, a ministry of hospitality to the homeless begun in 1985:

I came from a family that was poor and learned what it meant to be poor—the being looked down on, the crushing and so on. Then I became very angry at that and was able to work my way through university and entered into the corporate world and did very well. I climbed the ladder and got promoted and transferred. We were making good money by anybody's standards, with expense accounts and company cars. That was the goal, and a lot of it was probably based on my own anger—a way of getting even.

But during that process I began to read the Bible for the first time and simply took it seriously. I saw almost immediately that it had some profound things

---

[1]The following is excerpted from "God Has Lifted Up the Humble," *Urban Connections,* Vol. 4, No. 1 (April 1988), pp. 1, 3-5.

to say about the poor—the central themes of the Bible. Suddenly we said yes to this God. What that meant for us was to change worlds also.

So we as a family—Suzanne and I and our two young children—gave it up. We sold our home, and I quit my job. We began this intentional downwardly mobile trek to enter into the world of the poor, ending when we got to Roanoke two years ago with $200 and looking for a place to stay. I guess it was a conversion in a sense. I just saw that profit was not my god anymore—God called us to serve people and not profit.

Our life together is a reason for tremendous joy. The liberation that we see people experiencing brings us great joy. For example, Gail came to us homeless. She got a part-time job and was able to get a small room for herself and her son. But Gail exhibited so many beautiful qualities that we talked with her about coming back and working with us at Justice House. She agreed.

Gail is a person who had been told that she wasn't really that bright. She had had a child out of wedlock and the stigma that goes with that. She didn't think she could read well at all. Not too many Sundays ago, I asked Gail to read a devotion as we began our worship service.

What I had done was ask somebody who couldn't read to read a devotion. But Gail said yes. She asked Suzanne to stand with her. And Gail opened her Bible and struggled through that Scripture in front of our worshiping community.

Then she closed her Bible and began to tell how people could do it—they could read if they had a problem reading, etc. Her story gave people so much hope. That was our sermon—God had spoken to us. It took tremendous courage on her part.

Not many Sundays later Gail was taking a more active part in leading our worship. She opened her Bible and read in a strong, positive voice. We were all rejoicing together because she's part of our community. We're so happy at what we are seeing. I am convinced that can only take place in the context of a healing community. I can't tell you what that means—to witness that. Joy isn't an adequate word.

I often think about the Great Banquet, sitting down with Jesus with these folks. I will shout a shout that permeates the universe because that day will be so joyful—to see these people truly liberated.

On the other hand, there are those who will not participate in community. The community tends to police itself. Those few people who try to be something they are not find out that they are "in the light" and quickly go some place else.

The only intentionality we really express is being a worshiping community. We never have discussed, "How do we become a community? How do we live together?" In our worship services there are many people who offer prayers that say, "God, help us to live together," and "Look at the person next to you—that person is a brother or sister." Without that there would not be community. What binds us together is indeed the work of the Spirit.

A lot of what we experience can only happen in a worshiping community of the poor. We don't have to worry about the career—we don't know what that is.

That's a $10 bill for a few hours' work for somebody, and next week it's the plasma center.

The other day a person who is with us did some work and got paid $10. He came up to me a short time later and stuck his hand in my pocket—there was a $5 bill.

He said, "David, that's for you. Money scares me. I have to give it away as soon as I get it, because money should be used to help other people. I want you to have this because I know you need gas for your car."

In his comments I heard Jesus saying, "Make friends with unrighteous mammon." We struggle and explain that away and say, "We can be rich, but poor in spirit," and all these lies we tell ourselves. Here's a person, poor, with an expression of faith that is, to me, astronomical.

I think of my struggle when I gave up the job and the house. We make moves like that, and we say we've done something extraordinary. These folks do it as a matter of course.

On paper, we don't represent much, but what's happened in our midst and through us has had an impact on our area beyond anybody's wildest imagination. It illustrates the biblical truth that "God chooses the mere nothings to overturn the existing order" (1 Cor. 1:27). God's power is manifested through our powerlessness.

The resistance we have to entering the world of the poor is very much a spiritual battle, because that's where the power is. If we entered the world of the poor, we would literally see the world turned upside down. God's power would just explode. Our choice is whether we want voluntarily to become part of the reversal now.

People who have an interest in our work (who are affluent) come and visit and make some comments on how much they appreciate what we're doing. But they don't worship. They don't relate to us in an intimate way. The presence of the poor is a stumbling block. The reason some won't come and intimately relate when you have this gathered group of poor folks is that they feel downright uncomfortable.

It's a mystery to me, but the poor in the world today, in a sense, are Jesus. Matthew 25 really says that. So if we say, "I can't relate to these people," what we're really saying is we can't relate to Jesus.

The truth is, we have to see God where God can be found. I believe that if we're not with the poor, we're not with God.

Reflecting and Acting

Prayer and work for peace and justice are connected; through the outpouring of God's Spirit. God's people are given the power to do justice. But also, those who do justice are the ones who are able to worship God rightly.

Prayer gives power for justice. Read Isaiah 42:1-7. This passage does not use the word *prayer.* But it mentions that God has put the Spirit upon the servant of God. Prayer is not only conversing with God, but experiencing God's Spirit. Prayer is being in the presence of God. Prayer is allowing God's Spirit to rest upon us and inspire us to cooperate in the work God is doing in the world.

What is the work of justice to which God has called

the servant of God? Will the servant go about this work by using the power of violence? How will the servant accomplish justice?

Doing justice enables prayer. Read Isaiah 1:10-27. What is God's complaint against the people of Judah, who are compared to the people of Sodom and Gomorrah? What are their sins? What is God's reaction to their worship services? What does God ask the people to do in order to worship rightly?

FOUR

Conversion to the Kingdom of God

Dear Christian Friends in America:

I am writing to you about conversion, and what it means to be born again into the kingdom of God.

Does your church teach that a person must be born again in order to enter the kingdom of God? You have probably either been asked this question or asked it of someone else at some time. What does it mean to be born again? With millions of Americans now claiming to be born again, but national policies and public morality not looking very much like the values of Jesus, it seems as if the meaning of conversion, or being born again, needs to be reconsidered.

Thine Alabaster Cities Gleam

People are always searching for vision, and for power to fulfill their vision. Proverbs 29:18 says, "Where there is no vision, the people perish" (KJV).

The church, God's community of faith, should provide that vision for the world. But the church in America has largely failed to provide an energizing, exciting, and challenging vision to its people.

For this reason non-Christians—and even Christians— have looked elsewhere for the vision of the good life. In the United States the nation has stepped in to fill this gap through its educational, military, business, and political institutions. The content of the national vision varies somewhat according to time and place, but the central elements of it are fairly constant.

The name of the vision is "the American way of life" or "the good life." Its central elements are a very comfortable or moderately affluent standard of living, the conquest of natural and human obstacles (ene mies) by ingenuity and power, and unlimited growth of everything from the size of farms to the gross national product.

This vision includes, on the negative side, the focusing of all evil in communism. The loyalty of the people is rallied around the threat posed by the common enemy, communism. The national vision, or ideology, is expressed in songs of pride and visions of an eternal future for the nation: "O beautiful for patriot dream that sees beyond the years, thine alabaster cities gleam, undimmed by human tears!"

Along with a vision there must be power to implement the vision, or it is useless. Hence, human beings are engaged in a constant search for power. Finding strength in numbers, they link themselves in social organizations for power. But the church in America has largely failed in the matter of power as well as vision. The church has indeed maintained some power, but only by restricting its sphere of influence to that of the invisible. This is somewhat to its credit, for it means that the church continues to offer salvation from sin and claims the power of God to offer salvation by grace.

It is nevertheless to the church's monumental discredit that it has abandoned the economic and political spheres of daily life to the state. The church no longer addresses the first petition of the Lord's Prayer, "Give us this day our daily bread," to God. Instead, this petition for the necessities of life is addressed to the presidents of corporations and the president of the nation. And so we no longer depend on God for the securities of food, clothing, and shelter, but rather on cheap foreign labor and access to the wealth of the nations.

If enemies threaten this access, as they do, we have the "defense" budget and the Pentagon to take care of the communists. The reader can confirm this description by listening to the television preachers for two hours on a Sunday morning, "God will save us from our sins and nuclear superiority will save us from our enemies," they say. Unlike God's people in Bible times, we do not need the Lord as the stronghold of our life (Ps. 27), for we have the president, Pershing II, and we are getting the MX. God may save us from our own sins, but as for the sins of those who set themselves against us, we will save ourselves from them. Thus, the prevailing ideology of power in the churches of America is humanistic anticommunism. God is considered irrelevant to the supreme crisis of our age—what to do about enemies.

The Kingdom Vision

There is an alternative vision available to the church. God in mercy may forgive the church for not shouting it from the housetops, but it would take a remarkably good sense of humor or an awesome spirit of forgiveness to do so. God probably has both!

The church as the body of Christ is called to announce to the world what Jesus announced—the presence of the kingdom of God. The first public words of Jesus according to the Gospel of Mark were,

> The time has come. . . . The kingdom of God is near. Repent and believe the good news!
>
> (Mark 1:15)

The term *kingdom* may be translated "sovereignty" or "rule." All of these terms denote the authority of God, and they are broad rather than narrow terms. It is significant that Jesus did not come announcing the soul clinic of God or the new psychology of God. If he had done that, neither the Roman political authorities nor the Jewish religious authorities would have spent much energy opposing his mission. But Jesus came announcing a kingdom. The kings and presidents could not ignore that.

The vision for life represented by the term *kingdom of God* is set forth in the Sermon on the Mount. There Jesus spells out what it would mean for "God's kingdom to come and his will to be done on earth as it is in heaven," the awesome hope for which he taught his disciples to pray.

The kingdom vision in the Sermon on the Mount (Matthew 5—8) may be described in three parts, setting forth a born-again humanity, life in harmony with the created world, and a trusting relationship with God. These three, humanity, nature, and God, are the stuff of which life is made, and to see them clearly is to be grasped by an exciting vision for life.

A born-again humanity is the first goal and the first promise of the kingdom of God. In the Sermon, the Beatitudes (5:2-12) present a people-centered vision of life. The meaning of life is to be found in people. Not in the people of wealth, frivolity, pride, power, brutality, selfishness, rivalry, and wickedness who appear to run the world, but in the poor, those who mourn, the meek, those who hunger for justice, the merciful, the pure in heart, the peacemakers, and the persecuted righteous ones.

All of this turns upside down every vision of life which leaves God out. But it introduces a whole new set of possibilities for blessedness. Obviously, this is a vision which cannot be understood without the experience of conversion. The Beatitudes describe the characteristics of a born-again humanity.

The Sermon proceeds beyond the Beatitudes to describe the qualities expected of the "born again." The great, central command of the whole message of Jesus is found in Matthew 5:44-45 where Jesus comes to the climax of his revisions of the law and says, "But I tell you: Love your enemies and pray for those who persecute you, that you may be sons of your Father in heaven."

With this command Jesus directs all of the sovereign authority of God in heaven at the stubborn center of the human heart and demands change! That heart today, captive to the American vision of humanistic anticommunism or to a vision of revolutionary anticapitalism cries, "I won't! I can't! Enemies respond only to force. I have a way of dealing with them." But Jesus stands and waits for repentance. He waits for conversion. He expects rebirth.

Jesus called twelve apostles to live together as the firstfruits of the new humanity which he envisioned. In those twelve the church was founded. They gathered others into the fellowship, and marked their entrance into the community with the rite of baptism. This new social entity called the church began to think of itself as the body of Christ in the world, after the resurrection and ascension of the historical Jesus into heaven. The believers observed a common meal of bread and wine to remember the sufferings of Christ through which they had received forgiveness and acceptance into the new community. They accepted the way of suffering love as the form of their witness to the reality of God's love for all of humanity. In short, they embodied in their life together the vision of the new humanity which Jesus preached—the good news of the kingdom of God.

Life in harmony with creation is the second part of the kingdom vision. Jesus, in the Sermon, defines a life of simple wants and rejoices in nature's dependable adequacy.

> Therefore I tell you, do not worry about your life, what you will eat or drink; or about your body, what you will wear. Is not life more important than food, and the body more important than clothes? Look at the birds of the air; they do not sow or reap or store

away in barns, and yet your heavenly Father feeds them. . . .

And why do you worry about clothes? See how the lilies of the field grow.

(Matthew 6:25-28)

Twentieth-century Americans, trapped in consumerism and having an essentially exploitive relationship to nature, can hardly fathom such words. Neither, indeed, could most of the people who first heard Jesus speak them. But our hardness of heart takes nothing away from the wisdom of what Jesus spoke. He was proclaiming the vision of the kingdom of God. Visions stretch and test and challenge us. We, in the end, must decide which vision we will follow.

We can try for the world's highest standard of living, no limits to growth, nuclear power plants to generate electricity for our VCRs, and nuclear weapons to protect it all. Or we can go for life in harmony with creation, sustainable through simple wants and nature's dependable adequacy.

A trusting relationship with God is the third element of the kingdom vision. This is the foundation of it all. Simply put, it is a life of prayer, a life of quiet trust in God, communion with his Spirit in our hearts, and walking in the fellowship of his people. The prayer which Jesus taught in the Sermon invites us to lay all of our life before God. After expressing our simple trust by addressing the Creator of the universe as Father, and declaring the supreme worth of his hallowed name, we are instructed to pray: "Your kingdom come, your will be done on earth as it is in heaven." Everything that God wills for his created universe, from a bird singing its morning song to the presidents of the superpowers gathering in Geneva to discuss peace or annihilation is included in that petition. This prayer is not, "Lord, save some souls today," but, "Thy kingdom come." There is a difference. The church in America urgently needs to discover the differences.

A Different Form of Power

The kingdom of God vision of a born-again humanity, life in harmony with creation, and a trusting relationship with God cannot be realized without power. The kingdom will not come without the exercise of great power. But this power is not the power of wealth, pride, and violent force in which human nature naturally trusts (see Peter's conversion, 1 Peter 2—4). The kingdom vision calls for radical conversion not only of our ideas of the good life but also of our ideas of how to achieve it. We must be converted to trust in a new form of power. The kingdom of God is not only a new place to go but a new way to get there.

God stands ready in heaven to do what needs to be done on earth. But God cannot do it if we are bent on doing something else ourselves in defiance of God's sovereign rule and clear command. If we need salvation from enemies we can either pray that God will deliver us from the evil one's temptations to use the power of death to achieve that end, or we can plunge blindly on in our humanistic anticommunism, with visions of MX and High Frontier dazzling our minds. We can love our enemies or kill them. But we cannot do both. There is a choice to be made.

Bible scholars say that the first Christian confession of faith was the one found in Romans 10:9, "Jesus is Lord." In the secular world, the title "lord" was applied to the Roman emperor at the time, to denote the power and authority of his office. For the Christians, therefore, to apply the title "Lord" to Jesus Christ was an open challenge, in some ways, to the sovereignty of Rome.

There can be little doubt that some such challenge was intended by Jesus when he couched his message in kingdom language. The vision for a new life (which Jesus set forth) and the power to accomplish it were different from prevailing world views and ideas of power which Jews and Romans held. Consequently, Jesus did not hide the fact that anyone desiring to follow his way would have to undergo radical changes in their way of thinking and acting. So he compared that change to being born all over again.

Because the evangelical churches in America have retreated from proclaiming the comprehensive vision of the kingdom and limited their message to invisible things, the concept and experience of conversion have been sadly depleted. So people experience some kind of conversion and claim to be born again while they still hold on to the American vision of the good life and human ideas of power—values which are radically opposed to Jesus' message of the kingdom.

The answer to this problem lies in the direction of a more thoroughgoing concept and experience of conversion. There is, from Jesus' kingdom point of view, much reason for criticizing the popular evangelists and their call to be born again. The criticism is not, however, that they call people to repentance and rebirth. The criticism is that they call for so little repentance (change) and only a partial rebirth.

What is needed is a bold confession (in keeping with the first Christian confession) that the convert to Christ has accepted both a new vision with its changed set of values and a new sovereign Ruler with his different form of power. In our time and place the best translation of the early Christian confession that "Jesus is Lord" may be that "Jesus is President."

If God willed that the title of the strongest political authority in the world of ancient Palestine should be applied to Jesus, what reason is there to believe that he would not choose the title of the strongest political authority in our time to identify Jesus today?

To confess that Jesus is President would mean to acknowledge that Jesus is right about the human qualities which are blessed, including meekness, hunger for justice, peacemaking, and love of enemies; right about life in harmony with creation through simple wants and cooperation with nature's dependable adequacy; and right about a trusting relationship with God, including trusting God for salvation from enemies as well as from personal sins. And if Jesus is right about these things, it follows by implication that other sovereigns with contrary ideas about these things are wrong. There is a choice to be made.

Conversion to the kingdom of God is the kind of conversion which the church in America needs to proclaim. It is a conversion to a new vision of life and different form of power—the power of suffering love demonstrated by Jesus Christ dying for his enemies on the cross.

Experiencing the Letter[1]

"Worship is a pledge of allegiance," the experience of Mary Sprunger-Froese, Colorado Springs, Colorado:

I work with a Catholic-Mennonite mix of people living in a community to which I'm financially and decision-makingly interdependent. We run three "houses of hospitality," a soup kitchen and drop-in center and make efforts at resisting the militarism that feeds and pervades this city. The city is home for the Air Force Academy, Peterson Air Force Base, NORAD, Fort Carson, and a host of high tech industries dependent on military contracts. We count on the larger extended peace community in all this work. We are nurtured by their partnership, as well as leadership, in efforts with the poor and peacemaking.

Peter and I joined the Bijou community seven years ago, seeking to connect with the biblical "option for the poor" and mandate for making peace through life with a small group of kindred spirits. It's good to be part of a misfit remnant that offers glimmers of hope and meaning in the midst of individualism and profit making.

During and after college, international students educated me to how the American way of life effects poverty in their countries. I learned that the United States funded and trained torture groups.

By living in households with friends who had international experience and who challenged me on life-

---

[1]The following is reprinted from *MCC Women's Concerns Report.* Sept.-Oct. 1986 (No. 68), pp. 10-11.

style and war tax payment, I was (lovingly!) nudged into new awareness of how my choices affected others' opportunities. My parents encouraged service. Gerald and Mary Hope Stucky, missionaries in Colombia, were spiritual parents in their faithful example of continuing to question and to be open to change and growth.

When I went to seminary, one of my professors, Millard Lind, asserted that worship is political—a pledge of allegiance. This confirmed my suspicions that nation-states and their laws are often at odds with God's ways and that Yahweh's politics stand in judgment on every human structure and system.

I experienced church as community—being loved, challenged, counseled, and called upon by companion strugglers. That was no doubt the grace through which my path evolved. Partnership with Peter, also a grace that has come via the faith community, has involved a short stay with his family in Saskatchewan and our life in Colorado Springs.

Our Bijou community does odd jobs to pay our bills: lawn and yard work, house painting, cleaning jobs, commercial artwork. We charge according to our needs and the person's income, and always have enough.

A flexible schedule, nonpayment of war taxes, the comfort and security we as a community feel to each other and our commitment to our work, the riches of people with whom we work and play, dialogue with our opponents: these are some of the joys of my life. Difficulties arise in choosing which issues to confront, which endeavors to focus on, and how to maintain hope amid indications that poverty (of spirit, mind, and body) is escalating. The ideology of "salvation by the Bomb" is reducing people to robotlike responses.

My work deepens my faith in what Jesus was about, in what he invited people to live out—yes, people can together live in the rule of God, here and now. The work I'm part of is central, I believe, to the bringing together of all things in Christ (Eph. 1:10).

Reflecting and Acting

The Sermon on the Mount (Matthew 5—7) has sometimes been called the constitution of God's kingdom. It is a manifesto for life under God's government. It outlines a way of life for the community of those who seek first God's kingdom and God's justice. It tells us how to be subjects of God's government.

Sometimes we as Christians have read the Beatitudes so many times that they have become too familiar. To recognize how radical are the Beatitudes, how much in conflict with society's norms they are, look at their opposites.

The American Beatitudes. You will be happy if you never admit any weakness and always look as if you can take care of everything by yourself.

You will be happy if you avoid any situation that exposes you to others' suffering or that causes you to sacrifice or suffer or be sad.

You will be happy if you can get back at your enemies, even it means using hate or violence.

You will be happy if you want and get a lot of material things.

You will be happy if you demand perfection from

others and make your relationship dependent upon their performance. (I'll only love you if. . . .)

You will be happy if you keep on stuffing all your emotional garbage—your anger, your hurt, your sin—inside of you and never clean it out.

You will be happy if you stay out of sticky situations and let other people fight it out, even if one person is clearly the oppressor and the other the oppressed.

You will be happy if everyone likes you all the time; likewise, it is terrible if someone does something bad to you.

Jesus' Beatitudes. Now consider this paraphrase of Matthew 5:3-16. What does it say about citizens of God's government? How is it different from society's beatitudes?

How happy are the poor in spirit; they will be part of the reign of heaven. How happy are those who know they are needy, those who have the spirit of the poor, those who do not depend on their possessions or money or reputation or influence to get what they need. How happy are those who depend on God, for they are under God's rule.

How happy are the gentle; they shall have the earth for their heritage. How happy are those who use gentle means, who do not use violence to get rid of the wicked, but trust in God and God's ways to overcome evil. In the day of the Lord, the whole earth will belong to them.

How happy are those who mourn; they shall be comforted. How blest are those who do not hide their faces from the suffering of the world. God will comfort them.

How happy are those who hunger and thirst for what is right; they shall be satisfied. How blest are those whose greatest desire is for right relationships, for justice among nations and individuals. God will satisfy their desire for justice.

How happy are the merciful; they shall have mercy shown them. How happy are those who show to others God's mercy: the kind of mercy that sends the rain on good and bad, that loves enemies and prays for persecutors. Those who show mercy will also receive mercy. For if you forgive others their failings, God will forgive you yours.

How happy are the clean in heart; they shall see God. Yes, happy are those who have cleansed themselves of the barriers that lie between them and God or between them and others. Without those barriers, they can see God clearly.

Happy are the peacemakers; they shall be called the children of God. Happy are those who work to bring peace and wholeness and right relationships at home and throughout the world. In doing so, they become like children who are the spitting image of their parent.

Happy are those who are persecuted in the cause of right; theirs is the commonwealth of heaven. How it is a blessing to be persecuted for the sake of right and justice and peace! Those who do so follow in the footsteps of the prophets, in the footsteps of the apostles, in the footsteps of Jesus. How happy they are because they know that suffering and the cross are the way to resurrection and new life!

You are the salt of the earth. You are the salty minority that is poor in spirit, working gently and nonviolently, mourning with those who suffer, desiring justice. You are the salt of the earth, spread throughout society like seasoning, preserving the earth from decay and destruction.

You are the light of the world. You are a community of peace set on a hill. By your merciful love for enemies, by your purity of heart, by your peacemaking, by your suffering for the cause of right, you are light. You are light so that people may see your good works and give praise to God. You are visible communities doing God's work of love, peace, and justice. You are God's people in the world for all to see. You shine with God's light.

FIVE

Christian Peacemaking

Dear Christian Friends in America:

I am writing to you about the unique contribution which the church as a community of believers could make to peace between nations.

What is the role of the Christian community in peacemaking? Does the church have something to contribute to peace between nations as well as peace between individuals? These are important questions for people whose Lord and President is called the Prince of Peace. The world expects something of Christians in this matter, although on the basis of the record, it hardly knows what to expect.

Where Has Peace Gone?

The human situation is marked by conflict and strife from the closest relationships of marriage and family to the widest relationships of nations and continents. To find a reason for this we might look in many places, but let us look into our own hearts and at your own experience.

Although most of us live in families and neighborhoods where people surround us most of the time, we know what loneliness is. When the light is turned off at night, we are alone. When we sit down in the dentist's chair we are alone! And sometimes even at a party or in a crowd we feel quite alone. Why? Perhaps it is because we feel the need for an acceptance by others which we don't experience. And this need for acceptance is often sharp because we have trouble accepting ourselves at the deepest level. We find it impossible to feel as good about ourselves as we would like to.

This in turn is because we know ourselves so well. We know some things about ourselves which we would give anything to change, or not to know at all. The whole truth about ourselves includes some things which we have done to others that cannot be changed, but how we wish they could be forgiven! And there are in this category also, and perhaps especially, some things which we have done to ourselves for which we cannot forgive ourselves. In a rare moment of honesty we may even cry out in our souls, "Who can forgive my sin?"

All of this going on inside of us affects our relationships with others. We find in our hearts feelings of suspicion and mistrust toward people with whom we would like to be very close. Subconsciously we are thinking, "If they knew me like I know me, they would keep their distance. Perhaps they are keeping their distance. Yes, I know they don't trust me."

Anger builds inside as little actions or words are taken as insults or put-downs. Alienation and hostility set in. Tension mounts and estrangement escalates.

Peace is gone. Where has peace gone? Can it ever be restored? What would it take to restore peace, to reconcile differences, to recreate community of spirits and community of persons?

The big shots—the high and mighty, the chairpersons, generals, and presidents who plan wars and talk about peace—do not admit their own smallness and insecurities. But they snore and blow their noses like all the rest of us, and at some time, although probably it was a long time ago, they lay awake at night and asked, "Who can forgive me for my betrayal of the truth, myself, and my friends?" The peace of the world is destroyed first in the soul of every person. The wars of the world begin in the hearts of unforgiven sinners, and the experience of that forgiveness is the first step without which the wars will never be stopped.

A Peacemaking Community

Into this kind of world comes one named Jesus Christ. He speaks of peace, love, and forgiveness. He says that love must be unconditional, extended even, and especially, to enemies. And he forgives the people whose failed attempts to love others, and themselves, have left them broken and defeated. The Gospel writers tell the stories of many people who experienced this forgiveness. Their stories of release from sin have inspired faith throughout the centuries in people who have tapped the same deep well of forgiveness in the heart of God.

The beginnings of a new community slowly emerge around Jesus, as twelve men, some of them former enemies of one another and all of them rebels against the perfect good of Jesus, respond to his call to the kingdom of God. In this process we see Jesus breaking down walls of hostility between people by taking transforming initiatives of love toward them. He took a tax collector who served the Roman colonial power out for lunch and invited a Zealot revolutionary to join his community.

We will look briefly at some characteristics of his community, which came to be called the church.

First, it is a community which maintains peace by the practice of forgiveness. Jesus gave careful instructions for dealing with breaches of relationship in his community. In Matthew 18 we read his three-stage process for seeking reconciliation with a brother or sister who has sinned. It is clear that Jesus placed high priority on maintaining the internal integrity, or peace, of his community.

Second, the church is a community where economic justice is implemented. The prophet Isaiah had said that peace would be the fruit of justice (Isa. 32:17). The first communities of Christ's followers implemented radical liability for each other's needs by sharing what they had with one another (Acts 2:42-47; 4:32-35; 20:32-35).

Third, it is a community which prays about its enemies. After experiencing a serious denial of their "religious freedom" by government authorities, the disciples prayed about the matter. (This should not be taken for granted. American Christians don't usually pray about religious freedom; they fight wars and support arms races for religious freedom. The difference is striking.) When Peter and John were released from prison they took their case to God.

> "Sovereign Lord," they said, "you made the heaven
> and the earth and the sea, and everything in them."
>
> (Acts 4:24)

What follows in their prayer makes it clear that they believed that the Creator of everything could, and would, do something about the government authorities who were oppressing them. It was a different kind of response to enemies.

Brother Saul

Jesus' teaching of love for the enemy had an impact on his followers. This can be seen from one enemy's story in the book of Acts, chapter 9. The unique contribution of the church to peacemaking is clearly demonstrated in the process by which Saul, a bitter foe of the new Christian community, became a member of that community.

There was no doubt about how Saul felt toward granting religious freedom to the new sect called Christians. He opposed it so adamantly that he supported those who stoned one of those Christians —Stephen—to death. After that, he went to the high priest and obtained authorization to go to Damascus and arrest any followers of the way in the synagogues there. Those he arrested he would bring back to Jerusalem for punishment.

But a funny thing happened on the way to Damascus. Saul saw a bright light from heaven and heard a voice saying, "Saul, Saul, why do you persecute me?" The speaker then identified himself as Jesus, and went on to say, "Enter the city and you will be told what you are to do." When he was about to continue his journey, he discovered he was blind. His companions took him to Damascus, and for three days he remained blind and did not eat or drink.

At this point the Christian community had to make its response to this enemy, Saul. It was the classic situation. Saul was the enemy threatening death to the loved ones of the Christians—threatening, without a doubt, someone's mother and someone else's grandmother. The ethical dilemma for Ananias (see Acts 9) was clear: Should he take responsibility for the defense of innocent lives and attempt to kill Saul, or should he obey the teaching of Jesus to love his enemies?

You may object that Saul was no longer an enemy at this point, and that Ananias knew he was not. The text of the story gives the impression that Ananias did not know for certain where Saul stood at this time, but that he did know for sure that God wanted to use him to reach out to Saul on behalf of the Christian community. It was a tremendous risk at best.

Ananias was a person with the same fears, hopes, and possibilities as you and I. We could do what he did if we paid attention and chose to follow his example. Let us look at what he did.

First, *Ananias heard the voice of the Lord in a vision.* The Scripture describes Ananias simply as a disciple. But it was understood in those times (if not today) that disciples lived in communion with God. If God sent an angel or a vision, someone with an open heart would be ready to receive the message. As a first step in peacemaking, this is not at all to be taken for granted. We may say without fear or contradiction that few Christians maintain the openness of heart and the disciplines of spirituality which make the reception of a direct word from God a reasonable possibility. Lacking that, the rest of the peacemaking process is stopped before it gets started. Living close to the Holy Spirit through prayer is an essential qualification for peacemaking.

Second, *Ananias obeyed Jesus' command to love his enemy,* which came to him in the form of instruction to go to Saul and help him recover from his blindness. This instruction has in it the ring of the Sermon on the Mount: "Pray for those who persecute you." That is a command which most of us, put in Ananias's position, would prefer to obey at a safe distance from the persecutor. Of course, Ananias had the same thought, and even voiced it to the Lord, but he was still listening and the Lord had more to say to him. In the end, Ananias was persuaded. The Scripture says simply, "So Ananias departed and entered the house [where Saul was]."

The next thing that happened is a dramatic surprise which is scarcely equaled in literature, although our familiarity with the story weakens its shocking impact.

Ananias enters the house, lays his hands on Saul and says, *"Brother Saul!"*

That is it! The unique contribution of the church to peacemaking: *A word spoken to an enemy in love.*

"Brother Saul!" Of all the titles or epithets which Ananias might have used to open the conversation with this enemy of the church, he chose the word "brother."

Whether he knew that Saul already was a brother, or whether he prophesied that he would become one, is essentially beside the point. Neither the knowledge nor the prophecy would have been possible apart from the miracle of God's grace in the situation. But Ananias was a man in touch with God and therefore open to God's miracle. That made all the difference.

Third, then, in summary. *Ananias extended to Saul a transforming initiative of love.* His words to Saul extended to his enemy the possibility and the challenge of change, of transformation. One can think of many other reactions to Saul which would have stifled the possibility of change and snuffed out the expectation which God had put in Saul's heart. But Ananias seized the initiative in a tense situation and injected a possibility for transformation.

A Contribution to World Peace

The man Saul had much for which to be forgiven before he could find his place in the Christian community. But in that he was no different from the rest of us. As we said at the outset, we have all been tried and found wanting in the court of our own heart, so everything depends on what we do with that guilty verdict. We can place it before Jesus Christ and hear his words of forgiveness to us, his enemies, or we can try to hide it within ourselves. But if we hide it, it does not lie dormant there. It rises up over and over again to poison our relationships, to alienate us from others, and ultimately to destroy world peace.

The community of faith shares the forgiveness of Jesus Christ through acts and words of love. God works through people to reconcile broken relationships. So God used Ananias. But Ananias did not act alone. He was part of the community of disciples at Damascus, who supported him in his approach to

Saul. Today you and I are invited by God to live in community with forgiven sinners, from there to speak Christ's word of forgiveness and acceptance to others (including enemies), so making peace.

But the Christians of America and of the world have far to go before they resemble Jesus or Ananias in their love for enemies. The record of history shows the church all too often condoning wars and even starting them. Many of these wars have been between peoples and nations claiming to be Christian. So the Christians have not really loved *one another,* to say nothing of loving their enemies. The irony of Gandhi's observation is painfully clear: "The only people on earth who do not see Christ and his teachings as nonviolent are Christians."

Nevertheless, the past does not have to determine the future. Christians could create a different way. The challenge has been stated this way: "A modest proposal for peace: Let the Christians of the world agree that they will not kill each other."

Imagine a world in which Christians observed a covenant of peace among themselves—a simple covenant that they will not kill each other. A world in which Christians in the United States would neither threaten nor prepare to kill Christians in the Soviet Union and vice versa. Imagine 175 million Christians in the USA withdrawing support from military and industrial preparations to kill 75 million Christians in the USSR. Would that have an impact on world peace? Imagine something similar in Ireland, Uganda, Nicaragua, and South Africa.

Is this a proposal for the abolition of war? Yes and no. It is more precisely a proposal for naming the abolition of war a good thing and identifying a first step in that direction.

The first step toward the abolition of war will be to deny war its current respectability. War, like terrorism, will continue. But it must not continue under the banner of respectability, and by no means under the *church's* banner of respectability.

War may be inevitable, but it is not respectable. Rape, burglary, slavery, and adultery may be inevitable, but they are not respectable. Any nation or church which would declare them respectable would be considered outlaw. The first step toward the abolition of war must be to deny war its current respectability.

To take this step, the church must begin with itself. The best thing that the church could do to deny the respectability of war would be for Christians to agree that they will not kill each other. This could start a movement toward a wider agreement among people not to kill each other. But that, as in the history of infanticide and slavery, would be a result, not a precondition of the church's stance on the matter.

This modest proposal is an attempt to generate an internal discussion in the church between Christians who are committed to nonviolence and Christians who are not. This discussion has not been undertaken with genuine seriousness for centuries. Non-Christian religions and nonreligious peoples can only benefit from Christians talking with each other about a covenant of peace among themselves. Such a covenant will by its very nature spread to the protection of the life of all people. There can no more be a pacifist church which kills non-Christians than there can be sunshine which spreads cold.

When Ananias said "Brother Saul!" he modeled Christian peacemaking. His action fulfilled the command of Jesus, "love your enemies." Perhaps he saw it as that. Or perhaps he saw it only as the fulfillment of a covenant of peace with a fellow Jew. Either way, his action was filled with hope. Imagine a world in which all of the Christians have agreed that they will not kill each other.

Experiencing the Letter

In spite of the political differences between the United States and the Soviet Union, Christians in the two countries are finding ways to become friends. One of these ways is through the many tours to the Soviet Union. On these tours, Soviet Christians and American Christians can meet face to face and discover their common interest in peace.

This was the experience of Bill Reece, a Disciples of Christ minister in Wichita, Kansas, who, with his wife, Ginny, went on a three-week church-sponsored study tour to the Soviet Union in May 1987.

"Everywhere we went, in all the churches, they wanted to talk about peace," said Bill. "After one service, a woman came to talk to us, weeping and saying, 'We want peace so desperately. But we are afraid of Reagan and what he will do.' "

"The church in the Soviet Union cannot speak openly about the issues, but they pray for peace constantly. They can do that in the liturgy."

Christians ("believers," as they call themselves in the Soviet Union) are under many restrictions from the government. Formal Christian education for children is forbidden. Believers are less likely to get job promotions or educational opportunities. Yet, the churches are getting stronger. The seminaries have tripled in size in the last ten years. The church buildings are filled for worship.

In most churches, those who attend worship are mostly older women, "babushkas." But when Bill commented on that, one Soviet man told him, "There will always be babushkas."

Soviet woman can retire at age 50; the men at 55. So many people become active in church after retirement, when jobs and schooling will no longer be in jeopardy. But in other churches, there are also increasing numbers of men and younger families.

In all the churches, the Reeces found a warm welcome. Their train had arrived in the middle of the night, three or four hours late, in Tallinn, the capital of Estonia, on the Gulf of Finland. Yet, "here were all these Methodists standing on the platform holding bouquets and waiting for us," said Bill. "They had scheduled a special Monday night service for us. We were in charge of the service. There were more young adults and teenagers in this church than in any church we saw. The minister expressed frustration at not being able to leave the country for global church conferences. But he was happy that his daughter had just been accepted at the University of Moscow."

Many believers view with hope the new openness of Gorbachev's *perestroika*. Increasing numbers of Bibles are being printed and imported. So are atheistic materials, but one source told Bill and Ginny that few people are buying them. In fact, atheism is almost ridiculed now for having any ability to have a spiritual effect on the country. Together, Christians and Muslims in the Soviet Union outnumber atheists. Soviet Christians say that the communists did everything they could to stamp out the church, but the church is thriving.

Part of the Soviet urgency for peace grows out of their experience in the two world wars, when millions of Soviets were killed. In Leningrad are the mass graves holding 10,000 to 20,000 bodies each, people killed in the 900-day siege of Leningrad. People come daily bringing flowers and mementos. Newly married couples lay their wedding flowers on the graves. "The common people do not want the horror of another war," said Bill. "They talked to us about it everywhere.

"We went to a young people's art exhibit in Moscow and were stunned at the preponderance of religious and peace themes," Bill noted. "One piece of art was a magnificent bronze of Jesus on the cross with Mary bowing at the foot, and with a crown of empty bullet shells around his head. Another work of art represented Chernobyl with a rainbow over it—melting."

Even when Bill and Ginny left the tour and, bolstered with their small knowledge of the Russian language, found a man with whom they had corresponded, they discovered that he, too, was a believer. "When we got to Leningrad, he was at the hotel to meet us. After we got to our room, he took a cross from under his shirt and said, 'I am a believer.' "

Now back in the United States, Bill and Ginny have given a report of their trip to the Soviet Union in twenty-five American churches, mostly rural. "We do some dramas, some role playing. We show our slides. People are delighted to hear about the Soviet Union. One woman came to us afterward and said, 'I never thought I'd want to go to the Soviet Union, but now I think I'd like to go.' "

The joy of making connections between Christians in the United States and Christians in the Soviet Union was mutual. An Orthodox priest in the Soviet Union told the tour group after he had pronounced the benediction for the service, "Your visit gives me such joy I can hardly talk. 'There is one Lord, one faith, one Christian love.' I say that in every service. I will pray for you. Please pray for us."

Even at a large Baptist church where there was little chance for conversation, there was a great spirit of kinship, Bill said. "As we got on the bus after the service, the people came out and waved and waved at us. We had a lingering sense that we are brothers and sisters."

Reflecting and Acting

Learning about Christians in countries outside North America. Where does your church support church workers and missionaries? Mission agencies are almost always happy to send written materials or to loan slide sets or tapes about their work overseas. Be informed, so that your prayer can be more specific. Then pray for these Christians in countries that are "enemies" of the United States, or in places where the U.S. is funding one side of a civil war.

Imagine yourself and these Christians as fellow citizens of God's country, as brothers and sisters in

God's family. Pray for their health, for their families.
Pray that they may have productive work and a secure
and peaceful place to live. Pray that their faith and
your faith may be strengthened. Pray that no American will ever be asked to kill them in war. Pray that
God will show you how best to express your love for
them.

Read the story of Saul and Ananias in Acts 7:54—8:3
and 9:1-31. Put yourself in the place of Ananias and
think of someone who is your enemy. Perhaps it is
someone who you are afraid may hurt you or your
loved ones. Perhaps it is someone who has already
hurt you either physically or emotionally. How could
you get to the place where you could call that person,
"Brother" or "Sister"?

Forgiveness is not easy. Sometimes those who want
us to forgive make it seem too easy. They want us to
"just forget about it." But before we can forgive, we
need to recognize that there is indeed a problem. We
need to be honest with ourselves and with God about
how we have been hurt or threatened with hurt. In
Acts 9:13-14, Ananias was honest about his feelings
and about what Saul had done. Sometimes we need to
pour out our anger to God before we can forgive.
Then God may show us something new about our
enemy, or something new about ourselves. Perhaps
we, too, have hurt the enemy or others in a similar
way. Then, we, too, need forgiveness. So when you
pray, tell God why this person is your enemy. Tell
God how you are hurting.

Praying for the enemy is not easy. Often when we
pray for our enemies, we are tempted to tell God to
make them change. We could find it easy to forgive, if

we could have some sign of heart in our enemies. We want to see that they have changed for the better; then we will forgive. But that is not how God's forgiveness works. Romans 5:8 says, "But God shows his love for us in that while we were yet sinners Christ died for us." When we pray for enemies, we need to throw out all our bargaining. Instead of telling God how our enemies should change, we can ask God to fill us with love for our enemies even if they never change. Ananias had only God's word that Saul was to be God's instrument "to carry my name before the Gentiles and kings and the sons of Israel." Ananias was able to say, "Brother Saul," before he saw evidence of changed behavior in Saul. So when you pray for your enemies, ask God to work in their lives, but don't presume that you know better than God what that work should be or how your enemies will respond to God's work in them. Pray that you can be filled with God's love for your enemy even if your enemy does not change.

Forgive us as we forgive. The Gospel of Matthew offers additional commentary on only one line of the Lord's Prayer: "And forgive us our debts, as we also have forgiven our debtors. . . . For if you forgive men their trespasses, your heavenly Father also will forgive you; but if you do not forgive men their trespasses, neither will your Father forgive your trespasses" (Matt. 6:12; 14-15).

The gospel message of forgiveness, thus, involves not only God's forgiving us, but our forgiving those who have sinned against us.

If you want to experience God's forgiveness more fully, practice each day forgiving someone who has hurt you. Find a quiet place. Sit comfortably, and relax your body. Breathe deeply a few times, breathing in God's cleansing Spirit and breathing out any tension or anxiety. Bring to mind an "enemy," someone who has hurt you in some way. Bring to mind someone whose hurt to you is still causing you pain or keeping you from a right relationship with that person. Then with Christ's love and support, relive that experience of hurt or anger. Tell Christ how you felt then and how you feel now. Tell Christ what changes you would like to see in your "enemy." Tell Christ how you failed to be Christlike in the situation, how you could have reacted differently. Think of a time when Christ experienced the kind of hurt you experienced. What did Christ say and do? Then listen and watch, in your mind's eye, for what Christ says and does for you and for your "enemy." Let Christ's love pour down on you and your "enemy."

For deep hurts, you may need to go through this prayer several times. Or you may need several periods of prayer in order to get all the way through this exercise. The first time, you may only be able to get in touch with your anger or with your depression. You may find it helpful to ask another Christian to pray this prayer with you.

You will know that you have been able to forgive when you are able to be thankful for how you have grown from the experience, or when you are able to reach out to others in a new way. You may be able to talk freely with your "enemy" for the first time since the incident. The hurt may still be there, but it is not keeping you from loving others, including the one who hurt you. Sometimes people have discovered that, after they have forgiven a deep hurt, physical ailments get better or their relationships with everyone improve. Or they may suddenly be able to make a decision that they had long had difficulty in making. God does use our forgiving others as a means of blessing us in ways we had never imagined.

SIX

Your Vocation and God's Creation

Dear Christian Friends in America:

Millions of Americans feel as if they live a life without meaning in a world that is sick. The natural environment seems to be struggling to survive and the social environment is increasingly hostile to life. Even Christians sometimes ask themselves, "What is the purpose of this daily round of work, sleep, and eat?" Many people have no work, or jobs which are meaningless.

Many young people lack purpose. They wonder what, if any, their vocation in life will be. The church is all too often of no help. It offers religion as an escape, a ticket to heaven, an excuse to forget about nuclear waste, acid rain, and oil spills. When it does this, it is truly the opiate of the people, richly deserving the criticism it receives from honest pagans as well as its own children.

The Vocational and Environmental Crises

Further reflection shows, however, that there is

hope in the church. But before we get to that, we must look at what is wrong. The close connection between the vocational and employment crises in people's lives and the environmental crisis in their world is often overlooked. The environment is rebelling against what people have been doing with their lives, their time, and their energy.

The search for meaningful work has convinced our society that "getting a job" isn't enough. Many jobs are degrading to the persons who do them and to the environment which they impact. For Christians, the effort to add a "spiritual ministry" related to "saving souls" does not solve the vocational crisis. Defining the purpose of the Christian *only* as making converts does not adequately reflect the scope of God's agenda—to unify all creation in peace and right relationships.

While spiritual ministries are important, the environment, meanwhile, is staggering under a load of pollution, exploitation, and malignant neglect. Toxic waste, both nuclear and chemical, poisons the soil, the water, and even the air. Acid rain kills the fish in lakes. All of this is fueled by what may charitably be called mindless technologies and consumptive lifestyle. Less charitably and perhaps more accurately, they might be called blasphemous technologies and lustful lifestyles. The land is filled with information without wisdom, speed without direction, and growth without limits. There is an obsession for quantity without quality in everything from copulation to cars.

The passenger pigeon disappeared long ago. The most threatened species now is the human species. Human relationships are characterized by the cruel and unusual, from planned executions to nuclear terrorism (which is called nuclear deterrence to make it more acceptable). In the January 30, 1985, *Christian Century*, Raymond Lawrence addressed the problem of teen suicides. He proposed that

> These young people were dramatizing, consciously or unconsciously, the logical conclusion of commitments that have been made by our nation as a whole. I am referring to the manner in which we now tolerate the vision of world destruction in order to defend our national space and institutions. . . . We as a people have made it clear that we will parlay human life on Earth for the preservation of Western political and social order. . . . The six Clear Lake-area teenagers may well be like the canaries that miners used to carry with them into the mines because they died first in the presence of poisonous gasses. As more fragile, delicate beings, the young people succumbed [first] to the danger that threatens us all.

While the focus of our subject is not the threat of nuclear war, that threat represents the high (or low?) point of wasted human energy and disdain for creation. The teen suicides predict the shape of things to come unless we soon find another way.

Living in Relationship to Creation

Here the church can help—if it will. The biblical vision of God's intention for humankind living in harmonious relationship with creation is available to the church (e.g., Gen. 1-3; Ps. 104; Rom. 8). But it seems that the church, far from calling for a harmonious relationship with creation, has undermined and even denied that humankind lives in any necessary relationship at all with creation. The heresy of spiritualization has gone this far!

The creation story in Genesis, in contrast, says that humanity is created to live in harmony with creation. The Bible knows nothing of a right relationship with God that does not include a right relationship with creation. God's intention from the beginning was humanity living in relationship with the creation and the Creator: with land and mountains, oceans and skies, sun and moon, plants and animals, wind and rain. In this understanding *our vocation is to walk with God in gently tending his wonderful, strong, fragile, and enduring creation.* The meaning of our existence is found in this vocation.

The Westminster Confession said it well, "The chief end of man is to glorify God and to enjoy him forever." This letter is about how we are to glorify God and enjoy him in the concrete dailiness of this life and world where he has placed us. As such, this letter is also centrally about evangelism, because this is good news. But it is good news that calls for repentance (as all good news with biblical integrity does), because people are not going to begin living this way without radical change. They will indeed have to be born again. But that is what evangelism is about.

I should identify what is not included in this discussion of vocation. I have not developed the concept and ways of our direct communion with God, except as that is experienced through our interaction with creation. Nor have I included in this letter in a direct way our interaction with the human family, except as this family is included in what is implied by the word "creation." However, if you will pause to think about our direct communion with God and our interaction with the human family, you will realize that both are experienced to a very large extent through our relationship with creation. So even these are not altogether excluded from this discussion. I have intentionally focused the concept of vocation on the non-human elements of our environment in order to restore a biblical perspective on that. I have devoted six other letters to how we live with God and people within God's good creation.

We turn now to the essential qualities of living in a harmonious relationship with creation. These qualities must correspond to the being or the nature of nature itself. That is to say, we walk with God gently tending the earth on nature's own terms, because nature is the way God made it, and nothing changes that. We either cooperate with the way God made the world, or we wreck the enterprise. And therein lies the excitement of living, the joy of discovery, the possibilities for glorifying God—by reflecting in an accurate way what God has created, including ourselves. There are four qualities of creation by which we can guide our relationship to it.

First, *creation is wonderful.* That is, full of wonder. God called it good. The Bible is filled with the goodness of creation. The psalmists and other writers verbalized the wonder of sunsets, stars, snow, ants, rivers, mountains, land, fish, and people. We take it for granted that those rural people lived in significant conscious and daily relationship with nature, but seem to assume that modern man has no need for such mundane concerns. So evangelists and theologians today jet through the skies in 727s, eat processed food from plastic plates, and sleep in air-conditioned condominiums oblivious of the fact that their lives are totally dependent on the earth's thin layer of atmosphere and even thinner layer of topsoil. A first principle of good theology is that the essential, even though abundant, is not to be taken for granted. It is wonderful, for instance, that oxygen is present all over the earth! This is not to be taken for granted.

A sense of wonder before nature enlarges our concept of God and leads us to worship. It imparts that respect for creation without which science and technology become exploitive and deadly. It renews hope. The book of Job, wrestling with the terrible problem of suffering, ends by pointing the sufferer to the inexplicable wonders of creation, and offers the awe which this inspires as its answer to suffering. God asks Job,

> Does the hawk take flight by your wisdom
> and spread his wings toward the south?
>
> (39:26)

Job has no answer except to wonder at this and many similar questions addressed to him by God. A church, a theology, and an evangelism which is out of touch with creation, fascinated by human achievements, and blind to the majesty of God's universe, has lost an important gift for the person in pain.

All of science is nothing more than tracing God's footprints through the universe. Science creates nothing; it only discovers and rearranges. That is okay. It is a great enterprise, but it isn't much compared to what God did when he made everything that science looks at. Science and religion both discover some truth. Both know some things truly. That is why ignorance toward the created world is wrong and agnosticism toward God is wrong. But neither science nor religion knows everything, and that is why dogmatism is wrong. We should speak with certainty often, dogmatism never, and humility always.

The created world is wonderful. As someone said about fishing, it offers an endless series of occasions for hope. Artists and musicians explore the wonder of creation. Let us thank God for their call to live in harmony with nature.

Second, *creation is strong*. What force holds the sun on course? Who set the Rocky Mountains in place and carved a path for the Mississippi River? What strength sustains the swallow in its migration flight over thousands of miles each spring and fall? Have you tried to row a boat against the current, hold a wild horse, or stop the advancing light of the dawn?

The strength of nature is shown in its abundance, its resilience, and its healing powers. Its abundance produces glaciers from snowflakes and mountains from specks of dust. The reproductive spores of some plants number in the millions. The pollen of a cornfield and the stars of heavens are equally beyond counting.

Its resilience is seen in the endurance of plants and animals through vast extremes of temperature in the changing seasons, the many ways a rabbit can get into the garden you have fenced, and the purification of water from muddy rivers and salty oceans to fall again as fresh rain. Its healing powers show in the vegetation growing over the yellow soil of an abandoned building site, a forest recovering from a fire, and the desert blooming after rain.

But there are limits to nature's strength and resilience. Pollution, resource depletion, and over-population are names for exceeding those limits in various ways. This leads to consideration of the fragility of nature.

Third, *creation is fragile.* While the capacity of creation for renewal and healing is awesome, it is not unlimited. The passenger pigeon, for example, reproduced itself in amazing numbers, but still it was no match for the greed of humans. The atmosphere can absorb and dissipate vast quantities of smoke and pollution, but there are limits. We have tragically exceeded those limits with sulfur dioxide gas from burning coal. Acid rain is the result, killing the Black Forest of Germany and the fish in the Adirondacks. It is now beginning to affect streams in the Western states.

Love Canal in New York was the first massive ground water pollution case publicized in the United States. Now there are hundreds of sites where toxic chemical dumps threaten near-permanent pollution of subterranean water for miles around. Human greed —sin—is the cause of most of this. Changed hearts and lives are needed to provide gentle care for water and soil.

At other places in the world, technological intrusions into the environment have rendered land uninhabitable by humans. Nuclear bombs exploded in the

Marshall Islands have left a legacy of cancer and genetic mutants in the human population. Native Americans in northern Canada are losing land to coal strip mining and pipelines, like their American Indian cousins to the south lost theirs to sheepherders and farmers centuries earlier.

One method by which abortions are performed is by injecting a saline solution into the womb, rendering the environment lethal to the fetus. This kills it and causes it to abort. The fragility of fetal life requires an environment maintained within narrow tolerance levels of temperature, salinity, acidity, and nutrition. On a larger scale, planet earth is a womb within the body of the universe, surrounded by a thin layer of atmosphere and delicately heated by the sun. You and I are tiny fetuses clinging to the walls of this globe, sustained by the soil and air, the sun, trees, plants, and animals. To pollute, deplete, or destroy this environment on a small scale renders life unlivable for someone somewhere. To ruin the environment on a larger scale, as in nuclear war, is to abort millions of God's living children from the earth.

Fourth, *creation is enduring.* Many Christians are so used to thinking of the shortness of time, the nearness of Christ's return, the prophecies of destruction, and the bliss of the rapture, that they think of creation as anything but enduring.

However, we don't know how long it will be until God brings an end to history as we know it. We don't know. Jesus didn't know. And Hal Lindsey doesn't know. This is a fact. No amount of talking, prophesying, or speculating can change it.

Since we do not know how long we and our children are to live on this earth, we are obligated to plan for the long term. Anything less than that is euthanasia—pulling the plug—not on an individual, but on the race. We have no more right to dissipate creation if we are sure it is going to come to an end someday, than we have to dissipate our bodies if we know we are going to die someday.

The resurrection of the body is God's witness that the created world has an enduring future. Those who tamper with God's plan for his good creation place themselves under the judgment of the words of Revelation 11:18, "The time has come . . . for destroying those who destroy the earth."

Walk with God

In conclusion, the goal of life is not basically to get to heaven; it is to walk with God. Our vocation is to walk with God in caring for his good creation. The direction of God's saving work has always been toward this earth. Angels have come, prophets have come, and finally Jesus came. Taking souls from this world to heaven is not God's main work, nor ours. Our task is nurture, not transportation. We are farmers, not shippers.

"[Jesus] went around doing good and healing all who were under the power of the devil, because God was with him" (Acts 10:38). We will do the same if God is with us. Jesus was restoring people to health and life on earth, not passing out tickets to heaven. Heaven is indeed a future reality for Christians, but, in its emphasis on the future, popular evangelism has demeaned our task of earthkeeping as we walk with God. John saw "the Holy City, the new Jerusalem, coming down out of heaven from God" (Rev. 21:2), *coming this way.*

So enjoy the wonder, run with the strength, relax with the fragility, and live with the endurance of God's creation. Walk with God.

Experiencing the Letter

In the Old Testament, the Hebrew word we usually translate *peace* is *shalom.* Shalom does not mean just the absence of war or the absence of conflict. Shalom means not only peace, but health, prosperity, living in right relationship with other people, and living in right relationship with all of God's creation. In Hosea 2:18, God speaks to Israel of living in peace with both people and animals: "And I will make for you a covenant on that day with the beasts of the field, the birds of the air, and the creeping things of the ground; and I will abolish the bow, the sword, and war from the land; and I will make you lie down in safety" (RSV).

Christians in the Anabaptist tradition have tried to express this right relationship with all of creation through the principles of simplicity. Simplicity does not mean doing without, just for the sake of doing without. There is no glory in being poor. Simplicity means using only what we need of the world's resources so that others may also live. So simplicity is a way of living justly and in harmony with other people. Simplicity is also using only what we need so that the environment itself may continue, so that natural resources will not be depleted or irreparably polluted. It means living so that all kinds of species of animals may also live. It means living so that war and nuclear bombs will not destroy the earth as we know it. Simplicity means living so that life can continue.

For centuries, Mennonites expressed their simple lifestyle through farming and rural living. But simplicity is not just for farmers. It is for city dwellers, too, as the following stories bear witness.[1]

"To me, scriptural simplicity means using all I have, whether much or little, whether material, spiritual, or intellectual, in such a way that it is available to help others.

"We've tried to do as much as we could with as little as possible. Since Aaron had been teaching on a low-salary scale, his half-time employment during graduate school required no major adjustments. We've never needed all the money we had, so it was a delight to be able to help several young friends through school.

"We all like doing things rather than being spectators. One person's interest is enough to get us all to participate. We outfitted the six of us for backpacking by shopping at sales and making simple things. The cost was less than most shops charge for a single outfit. We enjoy free public lakes, parks, and concerts. Our four boys all took free music lessons at school. They bought and repaired old instruments, learning skills as they did so."

—Ruth Martin, Ephrata, Pennsylvania[2]

---

[1] These stories are reprinted from *Living More with Less,* by Doris Janzen Longacre (Herald Press, 1980).
[2] Ibid., pp. 90-91.

"When we last lived in Israel, an Arab woman made for me a long black-with-red embroidered *tobe*—the traditional dress of the village women. I decided that, having made the investment, I should really use the dress here at home. Long, loose, machine-washable and dryable, opaque, comfortable, and modest, this is my shopping-school-church-wedding-funeral dress! This summer, for the first time in over three years, I bought a dress of conventional make to wear on hottest days. I wore it once or twice, both times uncomfortably, and quickly changed back into my *tobe*.

"This gesture will surely not be taken up by many women. Most will not have the opportunity to get such a dress. But several people told me that because of it they were inspired to streamline their wardrobes drastically. Maybe sometimes it takes a far-out idea to help us move just a little closer toward a life of 'more and less'—more investment in the life of the kingdom and less preoccupation with what we shall eat and what we shall drink and how we shall be clothed."

—Miriam Lind, Goshen, Indiana[3]

"I don't let advertisers con me into buying those soft, strong absorbent whatevers. We use old towels, tea towels, tablecloths, sheets, and underwear for cleaning, dusting, and mopping-up operations. We tuck clean, folded rags into picnic baskets for cleanup jobs. A cloth or two in the car is handy for cleaning

---

[3] Ibid., p. 105.

the windshield or wiping the dipstick, as well as for bandages or wiping sticky fingers while traveling."
—Vivian Lautermilch, Calgary, Alberta[4]

"By the time we could afford a garbage disposal, our priorities had changed. We began to ask: Why spend money on another appliance requiring electricity and water? Why add to the city's waste-disposal system? Why buy commercial fertilizer for our garden while sending potential compost down the drain?"
—Rosemary Moyer, North Newton, Kansas[5]

"As a member of a citizens' group called Garbage Probe, I try to educate people about the problems of waste. This includes writing to all levels of government as well as to school boards and churches. I've also spoken to many restaurant owners and industrial executives about overpackaging.

"In my talks with dozens of groups I find children most receptive. The idea that every soda pop can takes ten cents of their allowance, or that Dad pays enough in taxes for disposal to buy a new bike each year or that it takes 400 trees a day to print our newspaper is really mind-boggling for them. Children can be taught not to abuse natural resources. Adult example is required."
—Carol Unruh, Waterloo, Ontario[6]

"One mother told me that she doesn't let her chil-

---

[4] Ibid., p. 158.
[5] Ibid., p. 165.
[6] Ibid., p. 279.

dren have birthday parties. This is her way of avoiding an overabundance of gifts.

"When our children have birthdays, our gift to them is the party and the cake. We organize special games and fun like baking cookies or stringing popcorn necklaces to take home. Sometimes we ask guests to bring gifts they themselves have made. A favorite one year was a fuzzy-wuzzy caterpillar in a jar!

"Rather than a material gift, an invitation for a mystery trip fascinates our children. Unknown to them until they get there, the destination may be a park, zoo, or swimming pool.

"Once our eight-year-old daughter came home from a party absolutely thrilled. The birthday child's mother had sewn cloth dolls before the celebration. At the party the children stuffed them and dressed them up with an assortment of remnants, lace, and other odds and ends. They took them home along with happy memories."

—Margot Fieguth, Mississauga, Ontario[7]

Reflecting and Acting

Read Psalm 104. Enjoy each image of the creation mentioned in this psalm, in which humanity lives in harmony with the rest of God's creation. Pray your thanks to God for all of creation, and listen to what God wants to tell you to do to live in harmony with this creation. What practical things could you do to help preserve the environment? What could you do to live so that other people in the world may also live?

---

[7] Ibid., p. 196.

Could you eat less, or eat fewer processed foods? Could you give up your plans to buy another electrical appliance? Could you give the money instead to a local food bank for the poor or to an international relief and development agency? Find a friend or a group of people with whom you can share these plans and help you practice them.

Read Revelation 21:1-4. The promise of Revelation 21:1 is not transportation from earth to heaven, but a new heaven and a new earth! God cares not only about heaven, the spiritual realm, but about earth, the realm we can experience with the five senses. Both the realm of the Spirit and the realm of the senses are gifts of God's goodness. If God cares enough about the earth to create a new earth in the age to come, then we ought to care about the earth we have now. It, too, belongs to God. God wants us to nurture it gently and reverently. The promise of the age to come is one of complete harmony in creation—no more crying or death or pain. Revelation 7:13-17 gives a picture of people who no longer have to suffer hunger or thirst or lack of shelter.

What can you do to live out the part of the Lord's Prayer that says, "Thy kingdom come, thy will be done on earth as it is in heaven"?

Love the enemies of the earth. When we have treated the earth violently, it has often reacted with violence toward us. What is true in human relationships is often true of our relationship with the earth. When we have polluted and poisoned the waters, they have become unfit to drink. When we have killed too many coyotes, the rabbit population has grown out of control and has sometimes eaten crops. Nuclear wastes generated today may poison the earth for our great-grandchildren.

Our violence toward the earth is illustrated by the way we have treated insect enemies. Our pesticides have killed insects in the short term, but the long-term results are often new breeds of pesticide-resistant insects. Other gardeners have found ways to repel insects without pesticides—planting marigolds or basil between tomato plants, for example. The insects are repelled by the smell or taste of the marigolds or basil and so leave the nearby tomatoes alone.

What next step could you take in loving the plant-and-animal creation?

SEVEN

Peace Church Evangelism

Dear Christian Friends in America:

I am writing to you about the troubled state of evangelism in America and the tremendous possibilities for an evangelism with biblical integrity.

Sincere Christians in the United States want to support evangelism. However, to do so places them in an extraordinarily difficult situation because the message and method of evangelism have been so seriously distorted. Popular evangelism as represented by the TV preachers has turned the good news into bad news. The time has come for another voice and another evangelism to make itself heard in the land.

Evangelism with Biblical Integrity

What is at stake in evangelism today is the gospel message itself. All of the basic Christian beliefs have been unmercifully assaulted. We must recover basic truths about God, Jesus Christ, the Holy Spirit, the kingdom of God, the church, and Christian vocation. For lack of a better term we are calling evangelism

with biblical integrity "peace church evangelism."
"Peace church" denotes the fidelity of some denom-
inations to the pacifism, the "love your enemies"
teaching of Jesus Christ.

Love of enemies is not the whole gospel, but, as
John Howard Yoder said, if another Christian truth
such as the obligation of faithfulness in marriage were
explicitly contradicted by most of Christendom, there
would be a faithful remnant somewhere which would
find its special calling in the proclamation of this
truth. So the peace churches have maintained the
truth that Jesus and his followers do not kill people
who oppose them—they love them.

A six-point outline of the message of peace church
evangelism follows:

1. *God, the source of salvation, saves from enemies as
well as from sin.* This truth must be rediscovered in the
Bible and proclaimed from the housetops. That God
saves from their enemies those who trust in divine
grace would be established if one key verse of the
Bible said it. In reality the Bible says it over and over.
No less than 88 psalms attribute salvation or protection from enemies to God. Psalm 37 says,

> The salvation of the righteous comes from the Lord;
>   he is their stronghold in time of trouble.
> The Lord helps them and delivers them;
>   he delivers them from the wicked and saves them,
>   because they take refuge in him.

(vv. 39-40)

Sin in the world has a twofold effect. Its effect in

our lives makes us sinners. Its effect in the lives of others makes us sinned against, or oppressed. To truly save us, God must be saving us from both of these effects of sin. The Bible, from God's deliverance of Israel from Egypt to the deliverance of the church from Herod (Acts 12), shows that God is in fact saving people from both sin and oppression. The TV evangelists spiritualize the gospel, declaring that only God can save us from our sins but that we must save ourselves from our enemies. This is humanism. The advocacy of military power against communism is humanistic anticommunism. The evangelistic message must declare a bigger God who offers full (not partial) salvation by grace.

2. *Jesus Christ is the disarmed one, who loves his enemies and commands his disciples to do the same.* Jesus Christ came into a world bristling with enemies. He came as a unilaterally disarmed child, lived a life of resistance to the powers of death and sin, did not resist his enemies who pursued him finally to the cross, and rose from the dead in vindication of this unusual way of life. The first command which he uttered, as Lawgiver in the tradition of Moses (and as the Son of God possessing all authority in heaven and on earth), was that people should love their enemies (Luke 6). This was the core of his teaching from beginning to end. It was the heart of his call to conversion, identifying the crucial point at which the human heart had to be changed, born again, redeemed, and restored.

The cross of Jesus was the specific historical result of his resistance to the powers of death and his non-resistance toward his enemies who were enslaved by the powers of death. By accepting the abuse of his persecutors and praying for them he broke the cycle of violence, tore down the walls that separated them from him, and made salvation possible. The resurrection is God's vindication of Jesus' way of living and dying. The good news is that the cross of Jesus and his resurrection can be experienced in our lives. Our cross is not essentially different from his. Ours also means suffering love for our enemies.

3. *The Holy Spirit is the life-giving breath of God doing justice for the oppressed.* Isaiah prophesied a time when the Holy Spirit would be poured out:

> Justice will dwell in the desert
> and righteousness live in the fertile field.
>
> (32:15-16)

Matthew and Luke saw Jesus fulfilling the prophecy that the Holy Spirit dwelling in Jesus would bring justice to the oppressed.

> I will put my Spirit on him,
> and he will proclaim justice to the nations.
> (Matthew 12:18; see also Luke 4)

Justice in the Bible means giving the oppressed poor that which is theirs by right—their due as human beings. Justice in Scripture does not usually denote punishment. It denotes giving an oppressed person that which is justly theirs.

> Woe to those who make unjust laws,
> to those who issue oppressive decrees,

> to deprive the poor of their rights
>   and withold justice from the
>   oppressed of my people,
> making widows their prey
>   and robbing the fatherless.

(Isaiah 10:1-2)

The Holy Spirit is not given to the church nor to individuals to give them a spiritual high or a good feeling while they ignore injustice and oppression. The Holy Spirit is given to send them into the world, empowered to correct oppression and establish justice. The former is religion as the opiate of the people, in the words of Karl Marx. The latter is religion as a liberating, saving power for which communism is no match.

4. *Repentance and conversion mean acceptance of the radical vision of the kingdom of God.* Jesus did not call people to a halfway conversion which left the materialistic, nationalistic, and militaristic theology of the converted person unchanged. Jesus did not call people to accept his radical alternative vision of the kingdom of God, set forth in the Sermon on the Mount. This vision cut across the grain of virtually every cherished value of his society. It does the same today. That may be why many evangelists have changed from preaching the kingdom vision to preaching salvation of souls and promotion of the American dream.

Evangelistic preaching with biblical integrity will put the emphasis where Jesus put it—not on escaping to heaven as a saved soul but on the doing of God's will on earth as it is done in heaven. This is the central petition of the Lord's Prayer, an enlargement of the prayer for God's kingdom to come (not, notice, for us to go somewhere to God's kingdom). All of this, of course, implies serious repentance and costly, radical conversion. To be born again could begin to take on a significant meaning.

5. *The gospel invitation is to join the community of forgiven sinners (the church) which loves its enemies.* The first thing that happens when a person accepts Jesus Christ and his kingdom vision is that they are adopted into the church—the visible, living, breathing family of God on earth. Salvation is not a vacation spot in heaven; it is a job assignment on earth.

The task of this community is to love. This is central. All else is incidental. It is to love, moreover, the unlovely and the hostile. Yes, the calling of this community is to love its enemies. This is rendered more possible by the realization that every member of the community was loved while still a hostile enemy. That is the heritage of forgiven sinners. This community continues the tradition of the church at Damascus in the book of Acts, which sent one of its members, Ananias, to accept its archenemy, Saul, with the surprising greeting, "Brother Saul!" Peace church evangelism explains that the church is this kind of enemy-loving community.

6. *Finally, peace church evangelism says that our vocation is to walk with God in gently tending his wonderful, strong, fragile, and enduring creation.* The goal of life is not to get to heaven, but to walk with God. Heaven comes later. God's intention, expressed in the Genesis creation story, is humankind living in relationship to creation. We are intended to walk on the earth, look at the sky, breathe the air, climb the mountains, wade

the streams, till the soil, enjoy the animals, and smell
the flowers. When we do these things we glorify God
and enjoy him, for God made this earth and lives in
it. But when we do not do these things as they should
be done, the water and air are polluted, the soil
erodes, the animals and plants die, and the earth
becomes uninhabitable.

Do you remember Job, that ultimate victim of
undeserved suffering? Job was shown the wonders of
creation to point him to God when his suffering
seemed too much to bear. A proper sense of awe at
the wonders of creation sustains life and restores
hope. God's creation is both strong and fragile, and
therein lies the challenge of using science and technology without abusing them. Creation is enduring.
We do not know its end point and we are obligated to
care for it and provide for its future just as we must
care for our physical bodies and not abuse or dissipate them.

Evangelism as Bad News

Having outlined an evangelistic message with biblical integrity, we will now describe the problem with
popular evangelism in America today. Needless to say,
there are exceptions to the characterization which follows and no evangelist or church whom it does not fit
need feel criticized. But thousands of Christians, and
perhaps just as many thinking unbelievers, will recognize the accuracy of this description and agree that we
are in a badly deteriorated situation.

First, popular evangelism has spiritualized the gospel. That is to say, it has departed from the proclamation of the kingdom of God and has turned to saving

souls. The difference between these two enterprises is so great that neither is recognizable by the other. A spiritualized gospel promises people peace of mind, freedom from guilt, and a home in heaven without changing the way they live in this world in any substantial way. Fortunately, there are exceptions to the general absence of changed lives. These tend to be persons whose visible sins are things like smoking, drinking, drug abuse, and sexual promiscuity. It is good that lives are being changed in these areas, but this leaves untouched many sins that are wrecking the world.

A spiritualized gospel omits the kingdom vision, divides soul and body in an impossible way, pampers the rich, blames the poor for the oppression they suffer, and makes going to heaven rather than walking with God the purpose of human existence. A spiritualized gospel can assume that everybody wants to go to heaven. It never stops to think that heaven is where God rules and that perhaps people who don't want to accept God's rule on earth (the kingdom vision which Jesus proclaimed in the Sermon on the Mount) might consider it a bad deal to have to live with it in heaven!

Second, popular evangelism has sold out to the materialism of the American way of life. The life of simple needs which Jesus described in Matthew 6 is not promoted because that would wreck the consumer economy if it ever caught on. Instead, conspicuous consumption is the projected image, and would-be converts are promised material abundance from God's unlimited storehouse if they will accept Jesus as their personal Savior.

It is ironic that a spiritualized gospel could be materialistic. The gospel of Jesus is radically material in the sense of embracing material things and the created world in keeping with God's intention. But the gospel of popular evangelism is greedy for material gain and excuses exploitation of creation's resources.

Third, and most damning of all, popular evangelism has made itself the handmaid of national aspirations rather than the expression of God's self-giving love. A fatal contradiction has been placed at the heart of evangelism in America. The good news that God loves the world so much that he is willing to die for his enemies on a cross has been linked with the bad news that America is going to stay strong if it has to destroy the world to do it. TV evangelists shamelessly advocate more military spending. A few years ago when President Carter invited some evangelical leaders to meet with him, the first question in the discussion period was from a nationally known TV preacher. He asked President Carter, "What are you going to do to restore America's military strength?"

The message of God's love delivered on the warhead of a nuclear missile! How long will God be patient with such blasphemy?

Patriotic songs are sung with more feeling than praises to God. Men in military uniform are honored on the same platform from which Christ's dying love for his enemies is extolled. The contradictions boggle the mind. The generals laugh and go on their nationalistic way while the preachers fall over one another to get into lockstep behind them. This is evangelism as bad news and America is suffocating in it.

In conclusion, peace church evangelism offers an

alternative to popular evangelism, which has spiritualized the gospel, sold out to the American way of life, and made itself the tool of national aspirations rather than the expression of God's self-giving love. The outline of an evangelism with biblical integrity has been set forth in the six points above and developed at greater length in the six previous letters.

I invite you to reread these letters, pray about them, and talk about them to discover whether God is calling you to this understanding of the good news.

Experiencing the Letter

The following is Lois Barrett's story of her conversion to peacemaking:

I was fortunate that my parents and the churches in which I had grown up had taught me something about racial equality and about helping the poor. But it had never occurred to me that the Christian faith might have something to say about war and the president sending money and troops to Vietnam. I never questioned the need for a strong military posture around the world. I remember being anxious during the Cuban missile crisis, wondering if there would be a tomorrow for me. But I didn't know there was any other option for international politics than war or threat of war. I just accepted what the society around me had told me.

My conversion to peacemaking began when I was in college. During my freshman year I had signed a petition supporting President Johnson's conduct of the war in Vietnam. By two years later, I was going to peace rallies and demonstrations. What had happened?

For one thing, I got some new information. Previously, I had not cared much about the details of the war. But then, I started hearing facts about the war, about the people of Vietnam. I started questioning why U.S. troops were there. I helped one of my psychology professors do the statistics for an attitude survey. The results of the survey showed that the more information people knew about the war, the more likely they were to oppose the war.

But just as important as the information was the way the war began to affect me personally. The need to decide about the war increased as I realized that both my boyfriend and my brother could be drafted.

In the process of my boyfriend's applying for conscientious-objector status, I discovered that there was a church that publicly opposed participation in warfare.

Through a one-year term in Mennonite Voluntary Service, working with and on behalf of the poor on my job, and for peace after hours, I learned to know people who connected peace with their faith. They did not assume that the president knows best. They had a heritage of spiritual and biological ancestors who had been persecuted for saying no to the government when the government opposed God's will. Their ancestors had been killed or driven from place to place around the world because they would not kill on behalf of the government. They were not anti-government. But they had given their allegiance to the God who so loved the world that he gave his only Son. They believed that the God who loves enemies wants us to love enemies, too.

Best of all, these people invited me into their

Christian community. They expected something to be going on in church besides having a number of individuals support each other's private worship of God. Relationships within the church were not just a nice by-product of coming to church, but important in themselves. They talked about working together, deciding together, church discipline, and sharing. That was good news to me, and I said yes to their invitation. That was peace evangelism.

But that has not been the end of my conversion to Christian peacemaking.

Through the experience of a personal crisis, I learned in the heart (not just the head) that God loved me, no matter whether I was good or bad. God could love me, even when some others did not. God could love me even when I had acted like an enemy of God.

I have been learning how to have conflict with others and still stay in loving relationship with them. It's tough, but sometimes I can do it.

I have been working with a local group of churches called Churches United for Peacemaking to educate other Christians about the gospel of peace: that God appointed Jesus the Christ to bring the message of forgiveness and love, even to die rather than hate enemies, that God raised Jesus from the dead, that salvation belongs to those who follow Jesus' way of loving enemies.

I have been learning (albeit slowly) how to depend on God to take away my anxiety and allow me to be calm in the face of angry or anxious people.

I have experienced release from depression and

physical healing after I have forgiven my enemies. God has worked with me in ways I never expected.

I have faith that God is going to keep on working with me in unexpected ways. I have faith that God's Spirit has more to teach me about the gospel of Christ, about peace, about justice, about living in harmony with creation, about prayer, about forgiveness, about loving enemies, about becoming a channel of God's grace for others.

My faith is a journey toward God. I've come this far by faith and I expect God to be leading me farther by faith.

Reflecting and Acting

Spend some time reflecting (perhaps journaling) on your own spiritual pilgrimage. Divide your life into four approximately equal segments. In each segment of your life, answer the following questions. What were the most important spiritual questions for you? At what points have you sensed God working in your life? Where has God worked in unexpected ways? What did you learn through those experiences?

As you reflect on the seven "Letters" in this book, how is God speaking to you through them? What new questions do you have? How is the gospel message of this book different from what you have heard before? How is God leading you in new ways? What is your cutting edge of faith?

What will you do to live out Christ's teaching of love for enemies?

Afterword

The *Letters to American Christians* themselves are also available in pamphlet form. They were written to be given away individually and used as conversation starters. Often, a single "Letter" received by a person is more likely to be read than a whole book.

For bulk rates, write to Herald Press, 616 Walnut Ave., Scottdale, PA 15683.

The Christian Peace Shelf

The Christian Peace Shelf is a selection of Herald Press books and pamphlets devoted to the promotion of Christian peace principles and their applications. The editor (appointed by the Mennonite Central Committee Peace Section) and an inter-Mennonite board represent the historic concern for peace within these constituencies.

For Serious Study

Durland, William R. *No King but Caesar?* (1975). A Catholic lawyer looks at Christian violence.

Enz, Jacob J. *The Christian and Warfare* (1972). The roots of pacifism in the Old Testament.

Friesen, Duane K. *Christian Peacemaking and International Conflict* (1986). Realistic pacifism in the context of international conflict.

Hershberger, Guy F. *War, Peace, and Nonresistance* (third edition, 1969). A classic comprehensive work on nonresistance in faith and history.

Hornus, Jean-Michel. *It Is Not Lawful for Me to Fight*

(1980). Early Christian attitudes toward war, violence, and the state.

Kaufman, Donald D. *What Belongs to Caesar?* (1969). Basic arguments against voluntary payment of war taxes.

Keim, Al, and Grant Stoltzfus. *Politics of Conscience* (1988). Traces the efforts of the historic peace churches to gain alternative service for conscientious objectors, 1917-1955.

Lassere, Jean. *War and the Gospel* (1962). An analysis of Scriptures related to the ethical problem of war.

Lind, Millard C. *Yahweh Is a Warrior* (1980). The theology of warfare in ancient Israel.

Ramseyer, Robert L. *Mission and the Peace Witness* (1979). Implications of the biblical peace testimony for the evangelizing mission of the church.

Trocmé, André. *Jesus and the Nonviolent Revolution* (1975). The social and political implications of the year of Jubilee in the teachings of Jesus.

Yoder, John H. *The Original Revolution* (1972). Essays on Christian pacifism.

——————. *Nevertheless* (1971). The varieties and shortcomings of religious pacifism.

For Easy Reading

Beachey, Duane. *Faith in a Nuclear Age* (1983). A Christian response to war.

Drescher, John M. *Why I Am a Conscientious Objector* (1982). A personal summary of basic issues for every Christian facing military involvements.

Eller, Vernard. *War and Peace from Genesis to Revelation* (1981). Explores peace as a consistent theme developing throughout the Old and New Testaments.

Kaufman, Donald D. *The Tax Dilemma: Praying for Peace, Paying for War* (1978). Biblical, historical, and practical considerations on the war tax issue.

Kraybill, Donald B. *Facing Nuclear War* (1982). Relates Christian faith to the chief moral issue of our time.

_____, *The Upside-Down Kingdom* (1978). A fresh study of the synoptic Gospels on affluence, war-making, status-seeking, and religious exclusivism.

McSorley, Richard. *New Testament Basis of Peacemaking* (1985). A Jesuit makes the case for biblical pacifism.

Miller, John W. *The Christian Way* (1969). A guide to the Christian life based on the Sermon on the Mount.

Miller, Melissa, and Phil M. Shenk. *The Path of Most Resistance* (1982). Stories of Mennonite conscientious objectors who did not cooperate with the Vietnam draft.

Sider, Ronald J. *Christ and Violence* (1979). A sweeping reappraisal of the church's teaching on violence.

Steiner, Susan Clemmer. *Joining the Army That Sheds No Blood* (1982). The case for biblical pacifism written for teens.

Stoner, John K. and Lois Barrett. *Letters to American Christians* (1989). Pithy essays about who Jesus really is and what his salvation has to do with the nuclear arms race.

Wenger, J. C. *The Way of Peace* (1977). A brief treatment on Christ's teachings and the way of peace through the centuries.

Yoder, John H. *He Came Preaching Peace* (1985). Bible lectures addressed to persons already involved in the Christian peace movement.

_____. *What Would You Do?* (1983). A serious answer to a standard question.

For Children

Bauman, Elizabeth Hershberger. *Coals of Fire* (1954). Stories of people who returned good for evil.

Eitzen, Ruth. *The White Feather* (1987). Based on the experience of a Quaker family who treated the Indians as friends and equals.

Lenski, Lois, and Clyde Robert Bulla. *Sing for Peace* (1985). Simple hymns on the theme of living with others.

Minshull, Evelyn. *The Cornhusk Doll* (1987). Tells how the gift of a cornhusk doll in a pioneer setting brought peace and friendship where there had been hatred and mistrust.

Moore, Joy Hofacker. *Ted Studebaker: A Man Who Loved Peace* (1987). A picture storybook of a conscientious objector who was killed in Vietnam while serving as a volunteer agriculturist.

Moore, Ruth Nulton. *Peace Treaty* (1977). A historical novel on the efforts of Moravian missionary Christian Frederick Post to bring peace to the Ohio Valley in 1758.

Smucker, Barbara Claassen. *Henry's Red Sea* (1955). The dramatic escape of 1,000 Russian Mennonites from Berlin following World War II.

The Authors

John K. Stoner lives in Akron, Pennsylvania, where he is currently writing and developing a ministry as a spiritual director.

John was born near East Berlin, Pennsylvania, in 1942. His education in the home and on the farm by his parents and eight siblings was supplemented by formal training in public schools and at Messiah College. He graduated from the Associated Mennonite Biblical Seminaries, Elkhart, Indiana, in 1967.

He was raised in the Brethren in Christ Church, an evangelical, pacifist denomination which grew out of a revival movement in eighteenth-century Lancaster County, Pennsylvania. He is an ordained minister of the Brethren in Christ. He was pastor of the Brethren in Christ Church in Harrisburg, Pennsylvania, from 1967 to 1975.

He was executive secretary of the U.S. Peace Section of the Mennonite Central Committee from 1976 to 1988, promoting peace through education, action, and interchurch dialogue. In the Peace Section he was active in New Call to Peacemaking, a cooperative venture of the Church of the Brethren, Quakers, and

Mennonites; the National Interreligious Service Board
for Conscientious Objectors (NISBCO); and the New
Abolitionist Covenant group, which called on the
church to go far beyond the nuclear freeze to urge the
abolition of nuclear weapons and war itself.

He is coauthor with Martin Schrag of *The Ministry of
Reconciliation* (Evangel Press, 1973) and numerous
magazine articles and pamphlets. He wrote the text
for the popular MCC poster, "A Modest Proposal for
Peace: Let the Christians of the world agree that they
will not kill each other."

John and his wife, Janet, have five children, two of
whom are adopted. Camping and hiking are favorite
family activities.

Lois Barrett is mentor (teaching minister) for a
cluster of house churches in Wichita, Kansas, known
as Mennonite Church of the Servant.

Lois was born in Enid, Oklahoma, and raised in the
home of a Christian Church (Disciples of Christ) minister. After completing high school in Sweetwater,
Texas, she graduated from the University of Oklahoma. She went to Wichita in 1969 as a Mennonite
Voluntary Service worker. It was there she became

acquainted with Mennonites and found a church that was clearly for peace in the world.

Since joining the Mennonite church, Lois has been a member of a Christian intentional community (1971-78), has served as associate editor of *The Mennonite* and news service director for the General Conference Mennonite Church (1971-77), and as editor of *The House Church* newsletter (1978-80; 83-85).

She has worked on peace issues through Churches United for Peacemaking, an organization of Wichita congregations working toward world peace (1983 to present). She also serves on the executive council of the Institute of Mennonite Studies, the Ecumenical Peace Theology Working Group of Mennonite Central Committee, and the Mennonite Confession of Faith Committee.

She is the author of *The Vision and the Reality* (Faith and Life Press, 1983), *Building the House Church* (Herald Press, 1986), *The Way God Fights* (Herald Press, 1987), *Doing What Is Right* (Herald Press, 1989), and numerous other magazine articles and pamphlets.

She is a graduate of Associated Mennonite Biblical Seminaries, Elkhart, Indiana.

She and her husband, Thomas Mierau, have three children, Barbara, Susanna, and John.